Using Supervision in Schools

A guide to building safe cultures and providing emotional support in a range of school settings

By Penny Sturt and Jo Rowe

Using Supervision in Schools

A guide to building safe cultures and providing emotional support in a range of school settings

© Penny Sturt and Jo Rowe

The authors have asserted their rights in accordance with the Copyright, Designs and Patents Act (1988) to be identified as the authors of this work.

Published by:
Pavilion Publishing and Media Ltd
Rayford House, School Road, Hove, BN3 5HX
Tel: 01273 434 943
Fax: 01273 227 308
Email: info@pavpub.com

Published 2018.

A catalogue record for this book is available from the British Library.

ISBN: 978-1-911028-91-8

Pavilion is the leading training and development provider and publisher in the health, social care and allied fields, providing a range of innovative training solutions underpinned by sound research and professional values. We aim to put our customers first, through excellent customer service and value.

Authors: Penny Sturt and Jo Rowe
Editor: Ruth Chalmers, Pavilion Publishing and Media Ltd
Cover design: Emma Dawe, Pavilion Publishing and Media Ltd
Page layout and typesetting: Tony Pitt, Pavilion Publishing and Media Ltd
Printing: CMP Digital Print Solutions

We are immensely grateful to the staff 'taking the leap of faith' by participating in the pilot we ran in schools – we value their input enormously. We would not have dreamt it up without encouragement from In-Trac colleagues.

We would like to thank Jeremy, Becky, Dom, Ben and Sarah for their support while we were writing this book.

We dedicate this book in memory of Andrew.

About the authors

Jo Rowe is an educational psychologist working for a local authority. Jo currently provides group supervision in a range of settings, and participates in group supervision with her team members in the Educational Psychology Service. Jo has 20 years' experience as an educational psychologist, with familiarity of working in a range of school settings and supporting children and young people with additional needs and school staff in these settings. Jo is keen to apply her knowledge and experience of group supervision to the wider school community. She recently extended this interest by researching the impact of supervision for school staff with a safeguarding role.

Penny Sturt is an independent trainer, consultant and registered social worker. Following her advanced social work training, which developed her interest in supervision, Penny has been delivering supervision training as an associate with In-Trac Training and Consultancy Ltd. Penny ran the pilot for schools having followed up requests for supervision training in schools. Penny has a long-standing interest in safeguarding and supervision across multi-agency settings. She has run training courses and consulted with health, social care and educational settings around supervision.

Contents

Introduction

Why now?

Schools across the UK, whether in the private or public system of education, are facing increasing pressures. While unprecedented changes in technology, ideology and globalisation have resulted in challenging school environments, these challenges have arisen alongside a decrease in the public resources that support children to make the most of their education. As well as changing expectations about how schools are governed, inspected and evaluated, there is also debate about whether support to schools (around student attendance and learning) should continue to be freely available from local education departments.

As a result of these pressures and changes, many schools are seeking supervision for staff to support them with the emotional demands they are having to deal with.

There are two main developments driving the push for supervision in schools: one, the increasing pressures affecting staff through recruitment, retention and their professional development (Harris, 2018; Asthara & Boycott-Owen, 2018), and two, the issue of safeguarding, as highlighted by Serious Case Reviews conducted on school settings in which staff have abused children (Wonnacottt *et al,* 2018; ITV News, 2018).

> *'All those working with children need to be equipped to identify potentially abusive behaviours, and to be empowered to report such concerns in an open and supportive environment where boundaries are explicit and adhered to.'* (Wonnacott *et al,* 2018, p272)

Staff value supervision for the emotional support it provides them, enabling them to do their job more effectively, and also it prioritises their developmental needs. For the Senior Leadership Team, supervision is a method of ensuring the codes of conduct and behaviour are maintained at the standard the school expects, and supervision therefore promotes safe cultures and high expectations of adult behaviour in schools.

'The way you look after your staff is the way you look after your students'
(Dix, 2017, p155)

Vitally important to staff is their need for emotional support to deal with the pressures they feel (see Chapter 5) – Penny has repeatedly been told how staff seek refuge in the toilets to regain their emotional equilibrium to continue their working day. The significance of staff toilets as 'safe spaces' in which to deal with feeling emotionally overwhelmed perhaps should be a wakeup call that schools need to attend better to the emotional needs of their staff teams. Hiding weakness from management has become a default (Chapter 6).

The most recent *Working Together to Safeguard Children* guidance available (Department for Education, 2015) and *Keeping Children Safe in Education* (Department for Education, 2018 (effective from 3/09/2018, before this point please refer to the 2016 guidance)) both reference supervision and support needed to deal with safeguarding issues in schools, however they do not clarify how, why and when. This guide therefore offers a model for supervision that answers these questions. Additionally, the model used in this book has been piloted in schools by the authors, found to be of benefit, and the key learning has been distilled throughout the guide – and in detail in Chapter 5. We need to be clear that supervision, as used in this guide, is for the support of staff and not the oversight of children.

There are two big questions which need immediate attention:

1. How will we find the time for supervision? This is often asked by the Senior Leadership Team.

2. Will this be a further way to demoralise staff? Frequently asked by junior staff.

The schools which participated in the pilot found that finding the time was not a problem once the Senior Leadership Teams were committed to taking action – they simply timetabled it in. Each school worked out their own solution about frequency and focus. For some, it was adding ten minutes a fortnight to see individuals, while others chose an hour each half term, or even termly. The time has to be manageable and meaningful. Having a structure and a clear focus helps to explain the purpose of supervision (see Chapter 5 for more information). Planned meetings decreased the number of meetings arranged in response to crisis, and it was possible to restructure existing meetings to fit better with a supervisory culture.

The integrated model of supervision used in this guide has 16 core components, described as a jigsaw, each of which need to be understood and used for effective supervision. The first four chapters of the book unpick these components.

- Chapter 1 finds out what the four functions of supervision are and answers the question, why supervise? It also models how the Teacher's Standards can be linked with the functions of supervision.

- Chapter 2 explores the impact on the 'four stakeholders' who benefit most from supervision.

- Chapter 3 introduces the method of supervision by using the four elements of the supervision cycle and applying it to various hypothetical school examples. This chapter also explores how the supervision cycle follows the functions of supervision and is of benefit to the stakeholders.

- Chapter 4 completes the discussion about the integrated model by stressing the importance of the four administrative cornerstones that underpin effective supervision. For successful implementation of supervision, it is essential that the Senior Leadership Team actively support building a culture of supervision and take responsibility for the policies and supervisory framework.

The second part of the book addresses the issues arising specifically in schools:

- Chapter 5 contains an analysis of what was learnt from piloting this model in schools working with students from reception to year 13.

- Chapter 6 continues to use the ideas gathered during the pilot in schools in order to think further about the challenges of implementation.

- In Chapter 7 the focus shifts on to assisting the Senior Leadership Team and governing bodies to think about how to go about building a culture of supervision in school settings.

Penny, with the benefit of many years supervision work in social care, was interested in looking at the impact that supervision could have in schools. She has been enormously assisted in pulling these ideas together by Jo's educational psychology perspective, as well as the experienced teachers, teaching assistants and others in school leadership roles who consulted us or who participated in the pilot.

This guide is the result of many decades of supervising staff and training others in supervision across social care, health, early years and, latterly, education settings. It has been (and surely will continue to be) a collaborative learning process.

The school leaders who participated in the pilot found consultation immensely valuable. This guide is designed to act as a consultative document in instigating supervision in schools using their feedback about what worked.

The final words about why schools are encouraged to try supervision come from a Designated Safeguarding Lead:

> *'I have felt the benefit of my own supervision to be very valuable and would like to offer my thanks for this. It takes an informed leap of faith, followed by sustained commitment in order for schools to recognise the benefits longer term. Having done this as a school, I am very willing to advocate the benefits to others.'*

Thank you for making the leap of faith with us.

Penny Sturt & Jo Rowe

Chapter 1: Why supervise and what does effective supervision look like?

Introduction

What is supervision? At its simplest, supervision is 'a professional conversation' (Department of Education, 2015). Teachers and other staff in schools are increasingly recognising that they do not have a structured framework for emotional support, in the way that other, similar professionals do. At the same time, increasing demands are being placed on schools to provide emotional support for children and their families. As a universal service, education is expected to meet the needs of all children, some of whom have very complex needs. Supervision is therefore a method of supporting staff so they can provide for the needs of the students and to build safe cultures for everyone in the school community.

The integrated model of supervision used in this guide has been applied extensively in social care settings and provides a framework that has also been tried and tested in a variety of school environments with the range of children in education.

Why supervise?

Staff in school settings have been talking about increasing levels of work-related stress, particularly, although not exclusively, those who have pastoral and safeguarding responsibilities (Asthana & Boycott-Owen, 2018). In the latest *Working Together to Safeguard Children* guidance there is an explicit expectation that staff in designated safeguarding roles are offered supervision:

'... a designated practitioner lead (...) for safeguarding. Their role is to support other practitioners in their agencies to recognise the needs of children, including protection from possible abuse or neglect. Designated practitioner roles should always be explicitly defined in job descriptions. Practitioners should be given sufficient time, funding, supervision and support to fulfil their child welfare and safeguarding responsibilities effectively.' (Department for Education, 2015)

Emotional Literacy Support Assistants (ELSAs) receive supervision as part of their contract of employment, as do staff teaching the Early Years Framework, where it is a statutory expectation (Department for Education, 2017, 3.21; Sturt & Wonnacott, 2016). However, the gap in providing support to other school staff with the emotional demands of their job roles needs addressing. Supervision is one way of filling that gap.

The model of supervision that has been developed for this guide complements existing models of performance management already used in schools. From their professional encounters with school staff, the authors' working hypothesis is that something similar to supervision is being offered in schools, but perhaps not in a way that is formally recognised or that has a theoretical base to provide its structure. It would therefore seem at present that teachers in need of support rely on 'asking a favour' of their colleagues or peers, or seek out a senior leader to manage their concerns. The model of supervision described in this guide instead provides a theory and practice that recognises and deals with the emotional stresses of a demanding working environment.

Supervising to safeguard

Students learn best (and staff work best) when they are safe, happy and challenged. Supervision is one method by which Senior Leadership Teams can help to ensure that they are kept that way. The expectation that students should be discussed with colleagues who have similar levels of knowledge and skill is essential in order to identify children at risk of harm, so that we might intervene early and effectively address their needs (Department of Education, 2015, paragraph 56).

Children are vulnerable to abuse because of their dependency on adults for their care and survival, and they are particularly vulnerable in group care situations (Erooga 2012; 2018). Recent Serious Case Reviews exploring abuse in school settings have highlighted the need for schools to establish safe cultures that protect students from staff who may pose a risk (Wonnacott *et al*, 2018). Erooga

(2012) summarised the twin purposes of policies and procedures when it comes to safeguarding children. First, they are designed to keep people who pose a risk to children out of schools by safer recruitment and formalised checking processes. This will not by itself remove the risk of future offending, but does act as a barrier. Second, policies and procedures foster safer practices within the school that encourage cultures of vigilance and awareness around individual staff members. This helps protect students from members of staff who:

> '... abused in organisational settings and yet appeared to have no known predisposition or motivation to abuse before taking up those posts.'
> (Erooga, 2012, p3)

In short, some people appear to abuse children because the opportunity presents itself. Schools therefore need to take steps to lessen these opportunities by strengthening policies and procedures and developing cultures of safe practice, as well as encouraging and supporting staff members to challenge each other's behaviour. (These issues are expanded on and their role in building a culture of supervision is explored further in Chapter 7.)

If a colleague is concerned about behavioural changes in a staff member or the way they are speaking about or dealing with a particular student or groups of students, how do they report those concerns in such a way that they are taken seriously? In their review of abuse in schools, Wonnacott *et al* noted:

> '...grooming or manipulating the school community was easier in situations where staff had not been equipped to recognise possible inappropriate conduct and unacceptable behaviours in colleagues.' (Wonnacott *et al*, 2018 p262)

Supervision can be an essential part of establishing and maintaining this culture of safe practice, which will safeguard both children and staff. It provides a structure within which staff can express their concerns, knowing they will be listened to and, if necessary, acted upon, and it gives them the encouragement to come forward in the first place: this is the person (your supervisor) you talk to about your concerns (as a supervisee).

Policies and procedures can be protective, but they are not protective by themselves. In order to be effective, all members of staff need to understand why they are required and how they contribute to a safer environment for students by taking part in professional conversations. Supervision works best when everyone in the school understands the reasons for it, including volunteers or parent-helpers.

What is supervision?

Framing supervision as a 'professional conversation', helps make clear what supervision is. Supervision is sometimes described as 'a one-to-one', a 'chat', or a team meeting. However there are big differences between 'chats' and supervision, and there is a need for a formal professional conversation about work.

Supervision discussions need to be more than 'a chat in the staff room'. They require clarification about the boundaries as well as what happens as a result of the discussion. Supervision is effective when there is a trusting relationship built between supervisor and supervisee and therefore some chat to build rapport and trust may form part of supervision. However, supervision needs to move on swiftly from chatting to tackle the main purpose of supervision, as outlined below..
The definition of supervision that is often used for school settings, which has been adapted from the work of Morrison (2005), states that:

> *'Supervision is a process by which one **member of staff** is given responsibility by the **school** to work with another staff member in order to meet certain organisational, professional and personal objectives, which together promote the best outcomes for **students**. These objectives and functions are:*
>
> 1. *Competent accountable performance (managerial function)*
>
> 2. *Continuing professional development (developmental/formative function)*
>
> 3. *Personal support (supportive/restorative function)*
>
> 4. *Engaging the staff member with the school (mediation function).'*

These four functions of supervision demonstrate why supervision is a helpful process.

Asking themselves the following questions can help staff to see each of these functions more clearly as objectives:

■ Are you doing what your manager thinks you are being paid to do? Everyone works better when they know what is expected of them – this is the 'managerial function'.

■ Could you improve what you are doing if given some training/different opportunities? This is the 'development function'.

■ What support do you need? What would help you emotionally to do your job better? This is the 'support function'.

- Whenever you are in school or on school-related activities, are you behaving and therefore representing the school as your manager expects you to? This is the 'mediation function'.

Each of these four functions is discussed in greater detail in the following pages. It is important at this stage to recognise that supervision needs to be a flexible response that caters to individual needs, and therefore in each supervision session the four aspects will not get equal attention every time. Being aware of the need to explore all four functions does, however, help supervisors maintain the boundaries around supervision and provides the structure that prevents the session simply becoming a 'chat'.

The managerial function

In order to do their best, staff and volunteers need to be clear about what they are being asked to do, in what manner, and when they need to do it by. Are staff doing the job expected of them? Supervision provides the means to discuss these issues, to establish accountabilities, and to clarify what supervisors expect from their staff team, such as which issues should be brought to a manager's attention immediately and which can wait. Supervisors need to know, for example, if a staff member has serious, immediate concerns about a student's well-being, but they could wait for supervision to discuss more effective time management techniques.

Members of staff also require feedback on their performance; they need supervisors to notice and recognise what they have done well, and to be offered constructive advice on areas for improvement. Some effective supervisors jot down their observations of good practice at the time they observe it, so that they remember to praise staff in supervision. Having good work noticed and acknowledged may make it easier for them to ask for help with tasks that feel difficult.

Thinking point

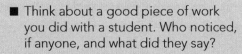

- Think about a good piece of work you did with a student. Who noticed, if anyone, and what did they say?

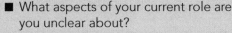

- What aspects of your current role are you unclear about?

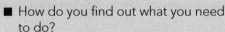

- How do you find out what you need to do?

The developmental function

The Senior Leadership Team, and perhaps the governing body/trustees of the school, need to know that staff are developing their capabilities and competence. In this ever-changing world of increasing expectations, it can be challenging at times to ensure that staff – and especially teaching staff – are knowledgeable, able to use their skills competently and have the requisite training to do their job, including working to the Teachers' Standards (Department for Education, 2013).

An important element of supervision is therefore ensuring that staff keep improving their skills, and it is the responsibility of supervisors to ensure staff have opportunities to achieve this. For example, staff are increasingly expected to be digitally informed, and yet this is an area which is constantly developing and evolving, requiring new skills. Supervision becomes a space to look for strategies to develop these competencies.

Another way in which the developmental function of supervision helps is by noticing and nurturing natural talents. Perhaps a member of staff has a flare for stimulating students' intellectual curiosity and enjoys finding creative ways of getting them learning. Supervision is the ideal time to encourage and nurture these skills, and perhaps move the staff member into a role where these skills can be used the their full effect – to co-ordinate the Education, Health and Care (EHC) plans in a SENCo role, perhaps, or as part of the pastoral team.

Finally, the developmental role can also be used as an opportunity to reflect on the value base that members of staff are using. How, for example, do they go about setting 'goals that stretch and challenge pupils of all backgrounds, abilities and dispositions'? (Department for Education, 2013).

Supervision is effective when staff are able to make links between their various experiences and decide what will help them improve their professional development. When a supervisee notices a training course or an interest they wish to develop, the supervisor probably knows they are being effective.

Thinking point

Having recently completed a learning walk with a newly qualified teacher, you were disappointed that none of the imagery on the walls reflected the culturally diverse group she is teaching. How will you raise this in supervision?

The supportive function

Supervision is a vehicle for ensuring that staff feel supported in their role, and it is this element that teaching staff in particular report they want from supervision.

While working with students can be immensely enjoyable, it can also be extremely exhausting. Staff have to help students cope with all kinds of things going on in their lives, including traumatic events – traffic accidents, the death of parents, loved ones or friends, as well as situations of abuse or neglect. Sometimes staff will be finding life difficult too. Staff need a confidential space to offload. Supervision can be that space to talk about how staff are feeling if they are working with distressed students or if they are overwhelmed by events in their own life. The skill of the effective supervisor is understanding the limits of the supportive function. Emotional support is crucial to allow staff to perform to their optimum capabilities.

Supervision is an opportunity to monitor the effects of the job and ensure they are coping and not becoming stressed by the demands of their work. It may equally be an opportunity to encourage creativity in trying new things out in an atmosphere of praise and encouragement. Supervision, if used effectively, ensures that staff remain responsive to their students' needs, not overwhelmed by stress or distress, and are able to seize opportunities for creativity. It should feel restorative.

Thinking point

- Think about a time when you were emotionally affected by a student's problems. Perhaps you were worried that they were being abused or neglected.
- How did you help them?
- What support did you need and who gave it to you?

The mediation function

Supervision is important not only in helping staff to be clear about what is expected of them, but also as a space to explore their knowledge and understanding of how their role fits with the rest of the school and other services provided to students, whether this is their role in their classroom, or in preparing students for a change of school, reporting to a child protection case conference, or reviewing an EHC plan. This is the mediation function. Staff in safeguarding roles, for example, may have information about the student's home life that may partly explain they are why struggling to settle to learn. Such staff have a key role in sharing this knowledge and helping other staff facilitate the student's learning. Depending on the size and governance of the school, supervisors may have a significant role to play in ensuring the expectations/policies of the governing body or trustees are understood by staff working on different sites.

There may also be times when staff are seen outside school – such as on school trips or in meetings, or when officially representing the school – when they have an important role in how the school is perceived by the local community. Supervisors are required to know how staff manage in these settings, and how they are behaving when they are representing the school.

The investigation into the well-known Southbank International School case drew attention to how William Vahey, the perpetrator of long-term abuse against boys, organised residential travel trips, set staffing levels, chose his favourite pupils to come on trips with him and was observed coming out of the pupils' accommodation, and yet other members of staff felt unable to raise concerns they had because of his relative power within the school (Wonnacott, 2018). With supervision providing a confidential and supportive space within which to disclose concerns, it is hoped that situations such as this are far less likely to develop.

Thinking point

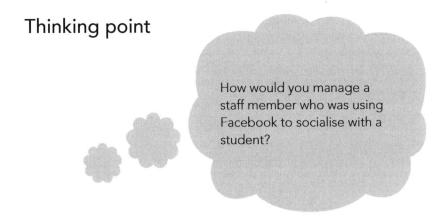

How would you manage a staff member who was using Facebook to socialise with a student?

Figure 1.1 summarises the Teachers' Standards and shows how well they match up with these four functions of supervision. Remember, there is a fluidity between all elements.

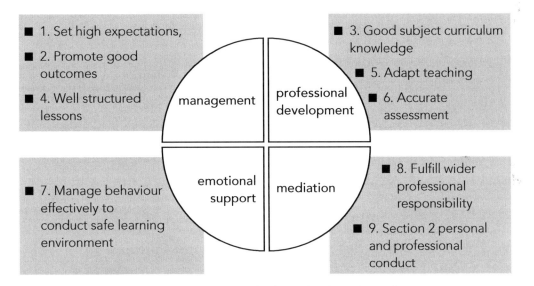

- 1. Set high expectations,
- 2. Promote good outcomes
- 4. Well structured lessons

- 3. Good subject curriculum knowledge
- 5. Adapt teaching
- 6. Accurate assessment

management | professional development

emotional support | mediation

- 7. Manage behaviour effectively to conduct safe learning environment

- 8. Fulfill wider professional responsibility
- 9. Section 2 personal and professional conduct

Figure 1.1: Mapping the Teachers' Standards to the functions of supervision.

Checklists that expand on each of these functions are included in Appendix 1 on pp108 and provide further clarity about how the functions differ.

Thinking point

Review the checklist in Appendix 1 and think back over your management of a member of staff over the last academic year:

■ How well did you balance the four functions at that time?

■ What was working well?

■ What do you need to learn to do better?

The difference between performance appraisal and supervision

Understanding these core components of supervision and why they are considered core will help schools work out what they need to include in their sessions and what they will need to manage differently because of their particular circumstances. This is discussed in greater detail in Chapter 6. Understanding the four functions of supervision helps to clarify what the purpose of supervision is, and what it is not. It also makes clear the boundary between supervision and performance appraisal at one end of the spectrum, and supervision and counselling at the other (see Figure 1.2, overleaf). Supervisors need to remain mindful that they need to offer emotional support and not just managerial input (at the performance appraisal end), and yet that their role is equally to ensure accountability and not only to support and encourage (at the counselling end). In short, supervision is about finding the balance between these two areas – supervisors are not counsellors, nor are they solely interested in the performance of staff. There will be times when a supervisor needs to stray a little further into the realms of counsellor, and times when they need to stray a little further into the field of staff/performance appraisal, but they should always be aware of moving back into the middle ground.

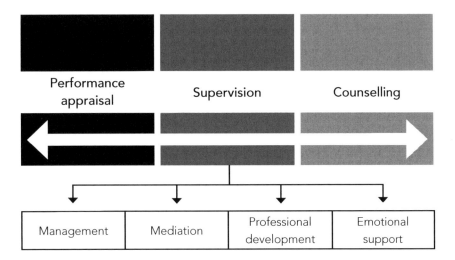

Figure 1.2: Performance appraisal, supervision and counselling. Created by Bridget Rothwell, In-Trac.

One way of thinking about this process as the supervisor is to imagine yourself with stakes set in the ground between supervision and performance appraisal, and counselling and supervision and with those stakes your role is to ensure you keep yourself in the middle supervision area. Place an imaginary rubber band to bind the stakes together. When you feel yourself being pulled into performance appraisal remember the importance of emotional support so that you effectively stretch the imaginary rubber band holding the stakes together but never lean so far over you only assess performance nor when pulled in the opposite direction do you become the staff member's counsellor. Staff need to know where the stakes in the ground are as well as the supervisor being clear about the remit of their role. There will be times when the rubber band is stretched as staff require frequent monitoring around a performance issue or more intensive support as they deal with a personal crisis. The metaphor of the rubber band is to demonstrate the need for flexibility while remaining able to pull back into shape as quickly as possible and not to pull so hard and often in one direction that it breaks.

These boundaries are important. As identified under the management function, there is a clear role for a formal performance appraisal process, at which the staff member's performance and competence is discussed with them and developmental tasks/goals identified for the future. And there will also be occasions when a member of staff's competence or capability raises concerns. In these situations, it is crucial that staff understand when their capability is an ongoing part of supervision (though never the sole focus), and when it is being formally appraised.

Formal appraisals can run alongside supervision (and can be carried out by the same person), but should be separate from the supervision process, and, again, it is important that the member of staff is aware of the difference. There may be developmental tasks identified as part of a formal appraisal process that supervisors and staff can discuss in supervision, although the formal evaluation of progress is conducted within the appraisal.

Schools tend to have a formal appraisal process with every staff member each term, and from working with schools, our suggestion is that this process could be performed annually instead. Each term/half term there is a supervisory meeting that discusses progress towards developmental tasks, offers emotional support and other aspects of the supervisory framework as described here. In the pilot conducted by the authors (explored in depth in Chapter 5), this approach was used by some schools with great success. Separating supervision from performance appraisal and asking how staff felt and how they were coping made them feel cared about and valued for the work they were doing.

The importance both of performance appraisal and of supervision needs to be understood. They are both necessary in order to build up a picture of how well staff members are working – for the staff members themselves, for their supervisor, and for the school in general. Therefore clarity about the boundaries between the two processes has to be maintained by all parties. It is not helpful for performance appraisal to be subsumed within supervision. Performance appraisal is a formal process. Monitoring the tasks identified from a performance appraisal may take place in supervision however the evaluative process remains separate from it.

Sometimes separating the roles of appraiser and supervisor helps, although how the findings from both supervision and performance appraisal are integrated, for the ongoing purpose of monitoring, has to be agreed by everyone involved.

Perhaps the 'myth' of supervision is that it is counselling or pure emotional support. This is not the case. It should definitely include emotional support as an integral part of it. However its focus is to support staff in doing the job specified in their job description and required by the school to the best of their abilities, including noticing and providing feedback when they do.

Supervisors as coaches or mentors

Sometimes the terms 'mentoring', 'coaching' and 'supervision' can get confused. A useful distinction between coaching and mentoring was defined by Hay (1995):

'A coach is an individual who helps another identify or remedy performance or skill deficit via modelling and rehearsal.'

'A mentor is the person who helps another learn from their experience in the workplace. It is a developmental alliance between equals.' (Hay, 1995)

It is perfectly legitimate that both these activities fit within the supervisor's role, and coaching and encouraging staff members' development are important functions of supervision. Skilled, effective supervisors will be able to decide whether they are coaching or mentoring the staff they are supervising.

Figure 1.3 shows how the coaching style a supervisor adopts may change as a staff member develops their expertise, from the supervisor being directive with a newer staff member (an NQT perhaps) to allowing a more experienced member of staff the scope to move themselves forward in developing their own potential.

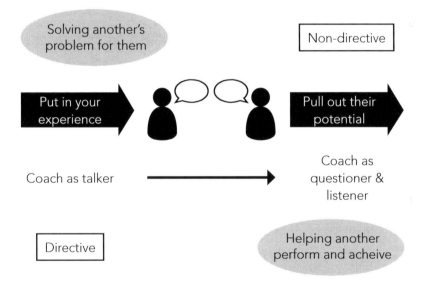

Figure 1.3: Developing coaching skills in supervision. Adapted with permission from Downey M (2003) *Effective Coaching: Lessons from the coach's coach* (2nd edition). London: Cengage Learning.

There is further discussion in Chapter 4 about how supervisors can adjust their coaching style depending on the competence of the staff member they are supervising.

Sometimes the supervisor may decide that involving others would be of benefit to a member of staff because an element that supports supervision might be better delegated to another; a member of staff may be asked to act as mentor to a new staff member joining the school, for example, or a member of staff who needs to be more imaginative in how they encourage students' learning could be coached by a member of staff who is more accomplished in this regard.

Accountability

In the context of supervision, it should be made very clear in each school where accountability lies, so that when there are important decisions to be made, such as whether a child is at immediate risk, for example, everybody knows who is responsible for making that decision. Arguably, it is this clarity and focus on accountability that defines it as supervision, as opposed to the simple 'chats' discussed earlier.

It is important to bear this in mind when a supervisor brings in another member of staff as a coach or mentor for one of their supervisees, and the 'chain of responsibility' and who is accountable needs to be clearly established. This needs to be clearly communicated to everyone involved.

Like nurseries and other community providers, schools often have close knit relationships with the community they serve, and between staff and parents. When the boundaries and responsibilities are not clear there is scope for children to be harmed (Wonnacott *et al*, 2018). Clarifying boundaries, including managerial accountabilities, and ensuring that all staff understand their responsibilities and that they deliver on them, is a significant part of supervision.

Furthermore, the location of some schools within small communities and the attraction of working in school settings for parents (who are juggling the demands of caring for children, and earning an income) means establishing appropriate personal and professional relationships is not always clear cut. Some staff working in schools are 'recruited from the playground' and begin their careers as parent-helpers/classroom assistants. Others continue their teaching career once they have become parents, by working in or near their children's school. This naturally creates an environment in which boundaries can become blurred and easily crossed, so it is important that these boundaries are firmly established and communicated, for teaching staff and other staff working in the school, for staff who are parents with children at the school, and for parent volunteers or those recruited into the workforce. Some of the specific challenges implementing supervision in this regard are dealt with in Chapter 6.

Supervision is vital for clarifying these boundaries, ensuring that everyone understands where they are, and for addressing issues when a person has, or is in danger of, crossing such a boundary.

Using the model of supervision in this guide ensures that, regardless of their role, everyone working in the school understands their task (the management function), how their role could expand (development function), who to talk to about their concerns (support function) and what the expectations of behaviour are within and beyond the school (mediation function).

The key ideas from this framework are highlighted in the discussion below as the focus of this guide shifts to how supervision happens (Chapter 2). The 16 piece jigsaw model advocated in this guide, which is built on extensive application in social care settings, rests on the importance of a **relationship** between the supervisor and supervisee. Relationships are at the heart of this model and blend with the ambitions of schools that promote **positive relationships** for children, with their families, their peers, the school they attend and the communities in which they are growing up. Schools are often in the centre of their communities and certainly students' sense of community and citizenship will often be reinforced by their school journey.

Understanding what the core components of supervision are and why they are considered core will help schools establish what is important to replicate and what they will need to manage differently because of the particular circumstances of their school. This is discussed in greater detail in Chapter 6. Supervisees have reported greatest satisfaction with supervision when it is based on a **trusting relationship** with a supervisor (Lambley *et al*, 2013).

For supervision to be taken seriously there has to be agreement within the school about the importance of supervision and how it will be given priority over other demands (see Chapters 4, 5 and 7). It will be challenging in the complex school environments, however feedback from those who have tried has been positive.

> '[supervision] *enabled me to recognise and meet the needs of my staff and ensure well-being was considered for all.*' (Supervisor feedback)

Supervision therefore, needs to be a formal process that is agreed and negotiated in advance between supervisor and supervisee. Sometimes the decision may be made that supervision will be a group activity, when a classroom staffed by a small group of staff for example, or where there is a shared purpose, like the safeguarding team (see Chapter 5 for ideas about what worked in practice). However there will be occasions when other demands intrude and deciding how those will be managed is also an important feature in making supervision effective. As can be seen in the chart below, there are arguments for and against every form of supervision and a flexible response will be required at times based on the supervisor's knowledge of the supervisee, their professional judgement of the situation and the level of risk management required. Formal, planned supervision clearly has the greatest benefits for everyone and is recommended as the most frequent form of supervision.

Advantages	Disadvantages
Formal planned supervision	
■ Permits advance preparation – agenda, relevant notes/ information can be brought, confidential space can be arranged, time allocated. ■ Both people (or group) prepared and have already thought about issues leading to better reflection. ■ Review previous decisions and ensure tasks allocated previously have been followed up. ■ Always recorded so clear continuity in the decision-making process. ■ Enables monitoring of performance. ■ Continuing professional development can be monitored.	■ Less responsive to crisis situations. ■ Some staff may prefer more informal meetings. ■ May increase anxiety in less experienced staff members.
Formal, less planned supervision (For example to debrief after a planned action, perhaps attending a review meeting).	
■ Planned and responsive to individual need. ■ Reinforces professional learning from planned supervisory session.	■ May need more time than allocated or ability to offer confidential space at time needed may not be there.

Planned informal session (for example when supervisor responds to request from supervisee for a meeting but sets a time).	
■ Allows some preparation for the issue to be discussed. ■ May be appropriately responsive to needs of student(s) and/or supervisee. ■ Nips issues in the bud. ■ There might be a quick solution to an issue that needs resolution.	■ Risks not being fully recorded and the issue might be only partially discussed. ■ Timing and confidentiality likely to be compromised.
Ad-hoc session ('Can I just have a quick word?')	
■ Suitable response to a crisis when decision needs to be made today. ■ Responsive to emotional needs of supervisee.	■ May not be recorded. ■ Some supervisees will use this as a way to avoid supervision. ■ Timing and confidentiality. ■ May not allow time for full consideration of issues and lead to poor reactive decision making.

In Chapter 4 there are pro-formas which suggest ideas about what could be included as the basis of supervision agreements which supervisors and supervisees could use in working together. Included within the pro-formas are ideas about how to manage unforeseen events such as absence or crises, and it is helpful to talk these issues through at the point of agreeing how to work together.

Thinking point

Looking at the chart above and thinking about the staff you manage:

■ Who is avoiding formal supervision (meetings) with you?

■ Why?

Conclusion

This chapter has introduced the importance of supervision and why it is a useful model for schools. It has provided a definition for supervision and explained the main functions of supervision. The importance of supervision and performance appraisal has been emphasised, together with the need for their interdependence.

Having addressed the importance of supervision, we move on in considering the core components. The following chapter moves into an explanation of the integrated supervision model by focussing on the people who are at the centre of the model and most likely to benefit as a result of supervision.

Chapter 2: Integrated model of supervision – a 16-piece jigsaw

Introduction

This chapter will explain the integrated model of supervision by looking at each of the 16 components that comprise the jigsaw puzzle, and why each is needed to make the integrated model of supervision work. This model is one which has been widely used within health and social care settings and has been adapted by the authors for early years and education settings. In this chapter, there will be a detailed focus on who can benefit from supervision, referred to in this guide as the **4Ss.**

What are the 16 pieces of the integrated model of supervision?

The integrated model of supervision is most straightforwardly conceptualised as four sets each with four components (see Figure 2.1). The purpose of this book is to explain the significance of each component and how to combine them for an effective model of supervision. From the previous chapter the reader is aware of the four functions of supervision; management, professional development, emotional support and mediation. At the centre of the model and key to making this model work are the beneficiaries, the people who gain value from supervision. In the context of education settings these are the **4Ss**; **s**tudents, the **s**taff, the **s**chool and the **s**takeholders. Using case examples the links will also be made between the Teachers' Standards and the functions of supervision, to highlight how supervision may be beneficial to the **4Ss**.

Linking the functions of supervision to the **4Ss** (beneficiaries) is the supervision cycle, the method by which supervision is offered. The supervision cycle has four elements to it; experience, reflection, analysis and action planning; and is based on Kolb's learning theory (Kolb, 1988). A more detailed examination of the supervision cycle is offered in Chapter 3. Significantly, and conceptualised as cornerstones of the model, are the elements around the outside; supervision policy, agreement between supervisor and supervisee(s), recording of supervision and its review. For supervision to be truly effective these four components have to be embedded into the foundations of supervision. This is because they explain the theory and describe the practice, so that staff members within the school know what it is they are agreeing to, as well as what happens as a consequence. Strategies for how to do this are discussed in Chapter 4.

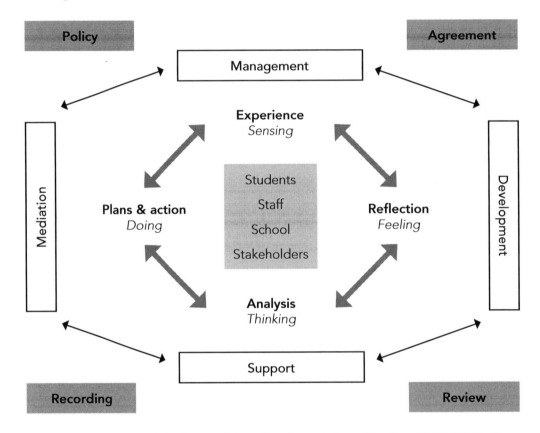

Figure 2.1: 4x4x4 model of supervision. Developed from Morrison T (2005) *Staff Supervision in Social Care* (3rd edition). Brighton: Pavilion Publishing and Media.

As each chapter unpicks a layer of the model the expectation is that how they relate to each other becomes clear. At each stage, there will be examples offered to explain how the model works in school settings.

The first chapter began to answer the question of 'why supervise?' in terms of how supervision can complement performance management techniques in ensuring staff have the competence and capability to perform to the best of their abilities. It emphasised the purpose of supervision. This chapter builds on these ideas about why we should supervise, by thinking about who else is affected when staff are not working optimally.

Thinking point

- How have you known if a colleague is underperforming? Perhaps a student mentions it or their parent or another teacher.

- What clues did you spot personally?

- What strategies did you use to tackle the issue?

Good supervision can benefit students, staff, the school and other key stakeholders such as parents and colleagues in other settings. It does this by being clear about the purpose of supervision, holding staff to account through the management structure; offering them opportunities to develop their competence; and supporting them emotionally as required; while also ensuring they understand how their role fits in with the expectations of others.

It is perhaps helpful at this point to use a couple of school-based examples and think through the impact on the **4Ss**. In the first example we discuss an issue in a lesson between students. In the second example we look at managing differences of approach in the class team.

Case example: Maria

Student Maria has approached Ms Styles at the end of her chemistry lesson in Year 11. Maria is tearful and alleging that a fellow student, Grant, has just put his hand up her skirt and inside her underwear.

Ms Styles has arranged to have an emergency meeting with Mr Lukas, the pastoral head.

Implications for the students

Maria needs to know that Ms Styles is taking her allegations seriously. She needs feedback. All students need to know what staff do when they raise concerns and that there are consequences for behaviour which is abusive towards others. Mr Lukas and Ms Styles need to think about the consequences for Maria, Grant, the rest of the Year 11 class and also other students in the school. Some of the questions raised by this example are around ensuring students are personally safe so they can take advantage of their learning environments, how students' concerns are managed so they continue to speak out and have trust in the staff team, how students' emerging sexuality is safely managed in school settings and does not compromise the learning experiences of peers.

There may need to be further investigation about whether Grant has behaved in this way to others and consideration of whether this is a child protection issue. There may be many possible explanations for Grant's behaviour; misunderstanding social and sexual cues, role models of men abusing power over women, sexual disinhibition. Or he might be being wrongfully accused. It is important for students' well-being that staff keep an open and receptive mind to what students tell them.

If there are implications for younger students and, especially if this is a repeat allegation, there will need to be consideration of what the next steps should be to manage Grant's behaviour safely, whether other students need safeguarding from him, including whether a child protection referral is required.

Implications for staff

Ms Styles may well need time and space to reflect on how the opportunity arose for Grant to put his hand up Maria's skirt and whether her teaching approach needs to change to lessen such opportunities in the future. This reflection is likely to include some thinking about what boundaries she needs to reinforce to make her teaching space a safe learning environment for students. She needs to work out what she needs to do immediately to make Maria feel safe and to be clear that there is to be no touching of other students intimately during school and never without their consent.

Ms Styles may be distressed by Maria's account, and this could stir strong feelings towards the students that she needs to accommodate. There may be policies and procedures that could assist her. She might be reluctant to resume teaching this year 11 class. Ms Styles may need some opportunities to rehearse what she says to show Maria's concerns have been taken seriously and to ensure that she is comfortable in using clear language about what happened.

Implications for the school

It is essential that incidents such as this are handled calmly and effectively. It is important that allegations around sexual incidents are taken seriously and responded to promptly. Should either Maria's or Grant's parents come to school it would be helpful for the head teacher to be able to reassure them about how the situation was handled and how their children will be safeguarded in the future. Similarly, other parents need to know what policies there are to keep students safe, what the expectations of behaviour for students and staff are, especially with regard to sexual relationships, and what the consequences of such breaches of behaviour are likely to be. The school and staff needs to be clear what its role in the child protection process is and what information can and cannot be kept confidential.

Implications for stakeholders

Parents sending their children to schools of course like to know that their children are safe, happy and learning. Governors or trustees are seeking assurance that this is true for students but also are committed to ensuring staff are competently working to the policies of the school. Ofsted and other agencies also expect that schools understand their responsibilities for safeguarding students; advising them appropriately when there are child protection incidents.

This hypothetical example has explored the implications for the supervisory meeting between Ms Styles and Mr Lukas in the context of an incident between students. The staff should consider their responsibilities for Maria and Grant as well as other students in that class and the rest of the school. They have to ensure that safeguarding and child protection policies have been adhered to, and agree an action plan to safeguard all students. Miss Styles should be supported in responding to a safeguarding challenge and reflect on her classroom management.

Case example: Myrna

Myrna is the teaching assistant assigned to a Year 1 class. The class teachers job share. Myrna is feeling stressed by the competing demands of these teachers. One teacher works with a plan and the other, with several years' experience, works more flexibly. Each week there is a disagreement about how to manage Ben, an autistic child in the class. Myrna has approached Ann-Marie, the line manager for this group of staff, for guidance about how she should manage the teachers' differences and her concern about the impact on Ben's enjoyment of school. She has noticed that Adnan, a child of asylum seekers from Syria who has recently joined the class, is also unsettled.

Implications for students

The inconsistent approach between the teachers could have a serious detrimental effect on Ben, who requires consistency to ensure an optimal learning environment. A behavioural specialist could be consulted to give Ben the best possible chance to succeed. The other students may well also be affected by the teachers' different approaches and lack of routine as well as the tension between the three members of staff.

As the issue has been brought to Ann-Marie's attention she could facilitate a group supervision session in order to agree a daily routine for the class and decide how the curriculum could be shared between each teacher. They should also discuss how the class should be structured to accommodate Ben's and also Adnan's specific learning needs best and what role Myrna should play in this.

The new daily routine and structure of the job share should be explained to the whole class and particularly to Ben to ensure that any student concerns are addressed and they are aware of the new plan.

Implications for the staff

Myrna is concerned about the students, especially Ben, and the affect the current dysfunctional job share is having on them. But she might feel that her opinion and experiences will be overlooked because of her lack of teaching qualification. She may also feel awkward being in the middle of two colleagues. She should be offered emotional support to explain the issues and be backed up by Ann-Marie.

The two teachers may feel stressed by the tension and uncertainty the job share is bringing to the class. They may also be aware of the effect on the students but unsure of how to resolve things or feel sure their way is the best way. Supervision should be facilitated in such a way that all staff involved feel listened to and their strengths and their role valued. The curriculum could be structured so that that they both feel they can play to their strengths, for instance one could undertake the regular assessment of literacy and numeracy and the other could develop spontaneity and creativity.

To make sure Myrna feels valued and to utilise her skills she could be given specific responsibility to prepare Adnan and Ben for their creative sessions, including spending more time with them in lessons to maximise their participation.

Implications for the school

It is likely that Myra or all the teachers are experiencing work-related stress, which can result in staff being signed off work. Supervision could prevent a situation from worsening to the point that staff resign or are unable to work.

The disruption and stress caused to Ben and Adnan by the inconsistent teaching could result in absenteeism, falling behind with work or even exclusion, and parents should be reassured that action has been taken to address the inconsistent lesson plans.

Implications for stakeholders

As well as parents, stakeholders such as governors are concerned with staff retention and ensuring the best possible outcomes for students, especially those with additional needs. Staff should be supported to reflect on their classroom management in order to achieve this.

Thinking point

Review the last difficult conversation you were involved in with either a member of staff or in regards to a student.

- Who else was being affected by the staff member's or student's behaviour?
- What happened as a result of your conversation?

Linking the purpose of supervision to the beneficiaries

Using these examples and the imagery from the previous chapter it is possible to link how the purpose of supervision improves the relationships between the people who benefit from it and also to demonstrate congruence with the Teachers' Standards.

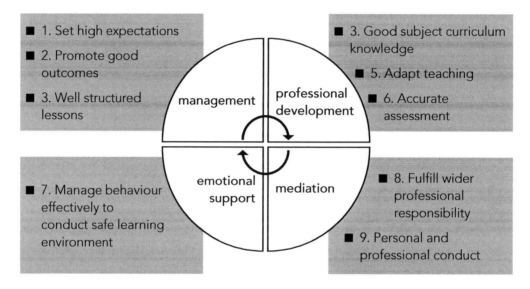

Figure 2.2: Mapping the Teachers' Standards to the functions of supervision.

The benefits of supervision in Case example: Maria

Supervision could be an important space for Ms Styles to seek **emotional support** and could allow her space to reflect on and learn about how to build her capacity for Teachers' Standards part 7 'manage behaviour effectively to conduct and provide a safe learning environment'. She may be able to reflect on what was it about her lesson that had facilitated this opportunity, for Grant to approach Maria and put his hand up her skirt, and what she might need to do differently. This may lead onto thinking about what expectations she had assumed the students knew (that this behaviour was unacceptable and breached school rules) that will need to be explicitly discussed with the class. This might result in some new **professional development** about classroom management and the need to adapt her teaching style and practice (parts 4 & 5 of the Teachers' Standards).

It might also provide a space to think about the wider school community and a method by which the pastoral head would be able to think about repercussions for other students in the school. This is the **mediation** aspect of supervision which also correlates well with number eight: 'fulfil wider professional responsibility'. It is also an opportunity for staff to think collectively and individually about their personal and professional conduct, part 2 of the Teachers' Standards. The discussion about how to feedback to Maria is part of what is expected about treating students with dignity. Supervision offers the space to prepare Ms Styles for how to do it effectively and respectfully so Maria knows she has been heard and taken seriously. Part of the strategy that will need to be agreed between Mr Lukas and Ms Styles could consider how Mr Lukas will respond if either Maria's or Grant's parents seek him out. In this way Ms Styles will know how the school will be supporting her in managing this issue.

The benefits of supervision in Case example: Myrna

Moving on to the discussion about the other scenario, where Myrna was concerned for Ben's learning, let's review how well the functions of supervision could be met in this example. After effective supervision Myrna may report feeling emotionally supported in a situation where before she felt she was subject to the whims of the teachers and worried about some students becoming increasingly distressed and hard to reassure. The **emotionally supportive** element might also mean that each teacher feels that their teaching style has validity which may have been recognised in what each offers to the students. Through the supervisory discussion it may have been possible to **mediate** a solution which worked for the Year 1 staff and thereby for the role of that class in relation to the rest of the school and their expectations of what students accomplish in Year 1. As part of negotiating this agreement about how they will work together there may have been a process of **professional development**, recognising where each currently has skills and competence but also the importance of being aware of what others are offering in the classroom to benefit the whole class. Ultimately Myrna and the teachers should leave supervision with an agreed **management plan** about how they would work together and what each person's roles and responsibilities were including how they would be held accountable for them.

Additionally, it is possible to extrapolate to the Teachers' Standards from this scenario. The resolution of the differences in teaching style and taking responsibility for differing parts of the curriculum facilitates accurate assessment of the children (part 6) so the students benefit, and it also leads to well-structured lessons (part 4), adaptable teaching (part 5) and safe learning environments (part 7) in which students and staff thrive. There is the additional benefit to the school of knowing that students are in an environment where there are high expectations (part 1), they are transparently monitored to achieve good outcomes (part 2) and led by teachers with good curriculum knowledge (part 3). All of which reinforce the message the governors need that they have employed staff able to fulfil their wider professional responsibilities by negotiating with each other and feeding back to parents or into professional plans with colleagues (e.g. EHC plans) (part 8).

By now the reader should be feeling confident about why supervision is needed in schools, and who benefits. Linking the purpose of supervision with the Teacher's Standards stresses supervision's relevance to governmental expectations. The next part of this guide is about how to carry out supervision, using the supervision cycle.

Chapter 3: The supervision cycle

Introduction

The supervision cycle holds the integrated supervision model together. It binds the centre of the model (the **4S**s, those people who benefit; **s**tudents, **s**taff, **s**chool and other **s**takeholders) to the outer rim (which are the functions supervision performs) by finding a way of allowing staff space and time in which to reflect on and learn from their working experience. This chapter will focus on the importance of understanding the theory that underpins the supervision cycle. By using case examples it will demonstrate the theory and highlight effective techniques in school settings.

The supervision cycle

The supervision cycle is a model adapted from Kolb's learning cycle (Kolb, 1988) for use in social care by Morrison (2005), Wonnacott, (2012; 2014) and in *Supervision for Early Years Workers* by Sturt and Wonnacott (2016). Kolb's work on how adults learn draws on the essential components of sensing, feeling, thinking and doing. In learning new skills there needs to be an understanding of the theory, to learn why what you are trying to do will work and why it might not, often by being shown. In learning any new skill there are emotional components; how you feel in trying something new, what support you may need and the opportunity to both try it out and think about how it could be improved. Importantly these processes need to be repeated and reviewed.

In schools the main learning issue in using supervision is about not rushing to solutions. There has been such a focus on time and performance management in recent years that finding space in which solutions can emerge is arguably the most rewarding, if challenging, part of using supervision in school leadership.

This book is using scenarios as a method for getting staff to understand the theory underpinning it. The supervision cycle is based on learning and therefore using examples of how people have learnt new skills emphasises the points made.

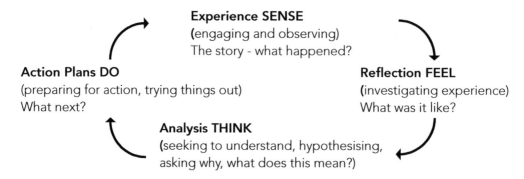

Figure 3.1: The supervision cycle. Adapted with permission from Morrison T (2005) Staff Supervision in Social Care. Brighton: Pavilion Publishing and Media.

Hetty, inspired by her daughter, decides she will take up tap dancing. Another parent accompanies her and they sign up for tap lessons with their children's dance teacher but at an adult class. The first lesson reminds them of childhood experiences of rubbing your tummy and patting your head, there is much laughter and no co-ordination. Neither is there a rush to judgement, the teacher praises, encourages and gives advice about technique (theory). The fun, companionship and promise of mastery is sufficient to motivate Hetty to return and persevere, gradually acquiring the skills sufficiently to perform in the next dance school show.

Contrast with this example;

Mike has been challenged by his mates to try unicycling. He's fit and athletic and knows he has good balance on a bike. In the context of his group of friends Mike is the qualified sports instructor and the expectation from them (and him) is that it will be easy for him to unicycle, he has transferable skills. Mike falls off repeatedly, is the subject of public laughter from his mates and walks away demoralised vowing never to try again.

What similarities and differences are there in the two examples and how may they be relevant to the supervision cycle? Mike had past experience which is relevant but not identical to the new skill he wants to learn. Mike has done what is often referred to as quick fix; he's assumed that he has all the knowledge he needs from riding a normal bike, as he has good balance and is athletic, that he can do unicycling without understanding how it works and differs from a normal bike. Yes, he had relevant past experience but he went straight to doing without any thinking about what he needed to do differently and how he might feel.

In a quiet moment Mike could be persuaded to try it again, if he asked for help from his peers or a trainer, in getting his balance on the unicycle and had a better understanding of the theory of uni-cycling. Mike needed emotional support and a better grasp of theory to succeed in riding a uni-cycle.

Reviewing these two examples show some important considerations for supervision. Hetty had the support of her friend and also found a supportive learning environment where there was praise and encouragement rather than ridicule. These examples also demonstrate that theory is integral to understanding, if you do not know what you are trying to do and why, you are unlikely to do it as well as you could. Learning something new risks exposing ignorance, no-one likes to feel foolish and therefore how well supported staff feel will affect their ability to expose their lack of knowledge and willingness to take on fresh ideas. A challenge in a performance-oriented culture is permitting mistakes, and yet learning is unlikely without making mistakes.

Schools should be places where students are safe, happy and learning. Supervision provides a method to ensure staff are too.

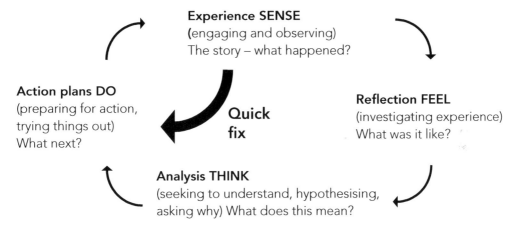

Figure 3.2: 'Quick fix' cycle – missing out feeling and thinking. Adapted and reprinted with permission from Morrison T (2005) *Staff Supervision in Social Care*. Brighton: Pavilion Publishing & Media.

The significance of these examples is the importance of every element of the learning cycle in order to learn effectively. It is possible for people to copy others and replicate what they have seen. However if they do not understand why they are doing what they are doing, they may run into difficulty if they encounter a different situation. For example, people who have learnt to ski without understanding how to stop.

Learning new skills takes time and practice. All elements need to happen for skills to be learnt, however they will not necessarily happen in the same order for everyone. As Kolb developed his theory he identified that people appear to have a preference for a learning style and therefore to start learning in different places on the cycle.

Thinking point

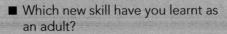

- Which new skill have you learnt as an adult?
- Think back about how you learnt.
- Did you jump right in?
- Did you wait until you were shown, did you need to know how it was going to work first?
- How did you manage your emotions, what helped you?

Mike from the previous example is an activist (sensing), he likes to learn by trying things out. Mike walked away from his experience with the uni-cycle demoralised and vowing to never return to try it again. However he needs to be helped to recognise that managing his emotions when he does not succeed is an essential prerequisite, learning to find out why what he did did not work, and then how to use his skills so he can transfer his existing learning about balance and technique are also required for effective learning. Hetty needs to be emotionally supported before she starts to learn a new skill, she starts the learning cycle as a reflector. For her the challenge at times will be about trying things out before she has perfected her technique.

In both examples of the learning cycle, the quality of the support affected whether the adult learnt their new skill. There is therefore a good fit with supervision. The aim of supervision is that staff understand what is expected as part of their job role, are able to deliver acceptable standards of teaching and pastoral care, that they question why things happen, know when and how to act on what they see within or outside the school and are able to reflect on and learn from their experiences with the support of their supervisor. Thus the supervision cycle matches the functions of supervision; management, mediation, professional development and emotional support.

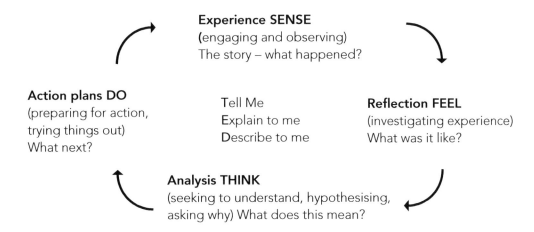

Experience SENSE
(engaging and observing)
The story – what happened?

Reflection FEEL
(investigating experience)
What was it like?

Tell Me
Explain to me
Describe to me

Analysis THINK
(seeking to understand, hypothesising,
asking why) What does this mean?

Action plans DO
(preparing for action,
trying things out)
What next?

Figure 3.3: The supervision cycle. Adapted with permission from Morrison T (2005) *Staff Supervision in Social Care.* **Brighton: Pavilion Publishing and Media.**

Supervision is a method of encouraging professional development. It mirrors a major task of schools, to facilitate students' development. Staff are expected to reflect on whether the student or class is making the progress they would anticipate and, if not, what reasons there may be, so they can be addressed and the student(s) assisted in moving on.

The diagram above features the supervision cycle, sensing, feeling, thinking and doing. Supervision is a collaborative relationship between supervisor and supervisee with the aim of empowering the supervisee to develop as a member of staff.

Experience/'sensing'

The experience part of the cycle helps the staff member and supervisor to gather the information about the student, their family/experience in school, the observations the staff member has made, comments they have heard from others. Its purpose is an information gathering process. From the supervisor's open questions (TED style: Tell me, Explain to me, Describe to me) staff are encouraged to think about all the sources of information they have about that student and their current situation. It is important that consideration is given to the perspective of others.

Reflection/'feeling'

Within the reflective part of the cycle is the opportunity to explore emotions. Students, especially traumatised ones, may well show a range of emotions that have a powerful impact on other people, without always being able to identify what is causing their distress. Staff members may have their own issues from childhood and occasionally those experiences may impact on a current situation. Staff need to be aware of how their past experiences from their own history are affecting their ability to think about this student's situation now. Members of staff will also be experiencing life stressors to varying degrees and need to be helped to remain alert to the impact of these issues on their performance, including their responsivity to students. This element of the supervision cycle is a space for the member of staff to reflect on their emotional responses to the work. The supervisor asks questions that prompt the staff member to delve into their emotional reactions to the students and how they are experiencing working in school. Probing in this way may also raise issues around staff member's views and beliefs which affect how they feel about undertaking all the responsibilities of their role.

It is also an opportunity to ask the staff member how the student is feeling, and whether they have noticed changes in how others are caring for or about the student which the student could have responded to.

Analysis/'thinking'

The analysis part of the cycle is seeking to make sense of the information and drawing on knowledge and theories that the supervisor and supervisee may have. There may be a range of possible explanations emerging and all may need consideration rather than only thinking about one. In fact encouraging staff members to explore a range of possibilities to explain what they have seen is important to ensure students are developing in their own unique way (part 5 of the Teachers' Standards – 'have a clear understanding of the needs of all students'). It is also essential that students' need for safeguarding is reviewed. Supervisors can use this part of the cycle to ensure staff members have up-to-date knowledge of the curriculum and know what they are looking for in relation to assessing students' learning and safety. Supervisors at this part of the cycle may find it helpful to use the perspective of another party to allow different theories or viewpoints to emerge. Staff need to participate in this part by explaining what they think is happening and in preparation for thinking about what they should do next.

Action planning/'doing'

When reaching this part of the cycle there is a great temptation to come up with a list of actions, however the key to successful professional development is enabling the staff member to work out their action plan from the questions the supervisor asks. There are several reasons for urging supervisors to resist from fixing the problems their supervisees bring. Firstly, staff need to develop their own problem-solving capacities. Secondly solutions which staff reach for themselves are more likely to mean that they will take the responsibility for doing them. Thirdly, and significantly, supervisors gain information about the competence of the staff member. Developing staffs' abilities to think through the consequences of situations in this way enables them to become more professionally autonomous and prepares staff for taking on additional responsibilities. It also lessens the demands made on supervisors to sort problems out.

Thinking point

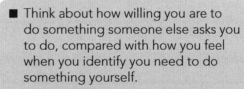

- Think about how willing you are to do something someone else asks you to do, compared with how you feel when you identify you need to do something yourself.

- Imagine being told to run an after school club compared with identifying a need and running it on your and your students skills and interests.

Supervision requires both participants to feel prepared and calm. How does the supervisor facilitate a learning environment for the supervisee? The TED questions that are used to facilitate student's learning are transferable to adult learning environments: Tell me, Explain to me, Describe to me.

Applying the integrated model

This sounds simple until supervisors try out resisting the urge to fix problems. Often when new to management roles there is a belief that being a manager requires coming up with the answers. This is hard to resist especially if staff bring this expectation with them, with statements such as; 'as my manager I expect you to tell me what to do'. Supervisors, remembering the functions and reach of supervision to others beyond themselves and their supervisee, can usefully spend time practising their skills in asking open questions.

The following scenarios allow supervisors to understand how the supervision cycle works in practice.

Case example: Sam

Sam is a teaching assistant and recently accompanied a group of Year 9s on a geography field trip. On the coach Sam noticed the geography teacher, Mr Philips sharing headphones with Jamila, one of the students. Sam is not sure why this has made him feel uncomfortable and has asked to discuss this in ELSA (emotional literacy support assistant) group supervision.

Suggested questions to ask about <u>experience</u> might include:

- Tell us more about this uncomfortable feeling?

- What made you uncomfortable about Jamila sharing headphones?

- How was Mr Philips towards Jamila?

- How did Jamila respond to Mr Philips?

- What else happened on the trip?

- Who else commented on this?

- How did the students behave on this trip?

- What surprised you about this trip?

Suggested questions to ask about <u>reflection</u> might include:

- Why did you feel uncomfortable?

- Who else was concerned about this?

- How do you think Jamila felt?

- How do you think Mr Philips felt?

- What was the impact of this behaviour on others on the coach?

- How do you feel about Mr Philips in general?

- Is there anything about this situation that reminds you of another similar situation? Tell us more.

Suggested questions to ask about <u>analysis</u> might include:

- What do you think was happening?

- Why were you uncomfortable?

- What impact has your gender had on how you perceived what you saw?
- What sense do you think Jamila had of this?
- What do you think Mr Philips' motives were?
- How did other students react, either at the time or since?
- What do you think you saw on the coach?
- How are things for Jamila now in the classroom/ school?
- How concerned would you have been if Mr Philips had been sharing headphones with a male student?
- How concerned are you for Jamila's safety? Why?
- How concerned are you about the school's reputation? Why?

Suggested questions to ask about action planning might include:
- What should happen next?
- What information is missing?
- What do you think you should do?
- What support do you need, and how are you going to get it?
- How urgent is this?
- What additional training needs have been identified?

Conclusion

If the supervision cycle was adhered to as above, the supervisory group has asked Sam to discuss his emotional responses to the situation on the coach and helped him to evaluate, by using his knowledge and observations, what it was about what he had seen that had made him feel uncomfortable. Sam has had an opportunity to think about whether he has seen or heard information from other sources which have contributed to his discomfort. He's also been asked whether there is anything from his previous experiences which is guiding him to check on possible sources of bias. Sam has been asked to think about whether there is an urgent issue which he needs to deal with and what support he might need to do so.

> ### Case example: Lyndsey
>
> Lyndsey is not learning as quickly as her peers. The SENCo has supported the class teacher (Year 1) by doing some focused observations of Lyndsey and has recommended that the school request a statutory assessment. Lyndsey's parents have refused.
>
> The SENCo has adjusted a learning programme for Lyndsey and six months on she and her teacher still feel that this is not meeting Lyndsey's needs. However the parents still refuse a request for a statutory assessment.
>
> The SENCo and the head teacher discuss Lyndsey's needs in supervision. They need to decide what the school does next.

To begin with the head teacher asks what is already known about Lyndsey and her <u>experience</u> of school and staff with her. Some example questions are:

- Tell me about Lyndsey.
- Tell me about her friendships.
- Tell me what you know about how she learns.
- What do we know about her parents?
- What other information do we know about this family?
- Describe her behaviour.
- What have we already tried?

Next the head teacher asks how staff and students feel, what their <u>reflections</u> might be. Note the possibility of checking out the views of a range of people to the same situation. For example:

- How are you feeling about Lyndsey?
- How do you think the class teacher feels about Lyndsey, her parents or the rest of her class?
- What impact is Lyndsey having on the class or the class having on Lyndsey?
- How are you feeling about Lyndsey's parents?
- How do you think Lyndsey feels about school?
- How do you think the parents feel about school?
- How are the parents feeling about Lyndsey's learning?
- Who else is worried about Lyndsey?

- What have other staff noticed about Lyndsey?

- How many other children have you a similar concern about their learning? How is this similar to or different from Lyndsey?

The next phase of the supervision cycle is to <u>analyse</u> the issue looking for understanding of the situation:

- Why is Lyndsey not learning?

- What is needed to help her learn?

- Why are the parents unable to work with the school?

- How concerned are you about Lyndsey and why?

- What other reasons could be contributing?

- What is working well in this class and why?

- How well do you think the class teacher is managing the class needs, including Lyndsey's?

- How well are other children in this class learning?

- What support has been offered?

- Why hasn't it worked?

Following on from this is what should happen next, deciding on what should be the next steps (<u>action plan</u>)? This is the most difficult part of the cycle for supervisors as they will usually have begun to formulate their own solution and need to wait calmly to see if the supervisee can find their own. However the concluding part of the supervision cycle is an effective way of monitoring professional development. The following are useful open questions for this stage:

- What should happen next for Lyndsey?

- What should happen next for the class teacher?

- What should happen next for Lyndsey's parents?

- Who should do what?

- Who else needs to be consulted?

- What support will be needed and for whom?

- How will we recognise progress?

- When are we going to review this?

Conclusion

The head teacher and SENCo in this scenario should have reached a plan about how they intend to take forward Lyndsey's learning needs, how to involve her parents and what the next steps could be. That plan should involve checking how well the rest of the class are learning and whether there are known issues regarding what the class teacher is doing that are impeding Lyndsey or other students from learning. The plan should have detail about what is expected, what the aims of the plan are and how long before it will be reviewed. These should meet the management functions of supervision. Throughout there has been attention to the emotional needs of the student(s), staff and others in the school including what support the SENCo may need with this particular situation. Because of the SENCo's role across the school there was some discussion about how typical or not the dilemmas around Lyndsey were and how to use the support of the special education needs and disability service, fulfilling the mediation element of supervision. It is possible that some development tasks around facilitating parents' involvement to support the student's learning have been identified within the discussion.

These scenarios have been used to introduce how open questions facilitate using the supervision cycle applied to hypothetical situations. Some ideas of effective questions to use at the various stages of the cycle are included in Appendix 2.

Thinking point

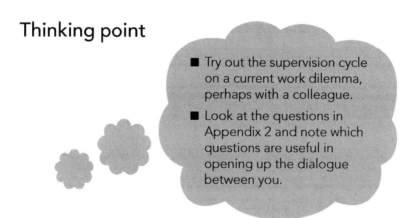

- Try out the supervision cycle on a current work dilemma, perhaps with a colleague.
- Look at the questions in Appendix 2 and note which questions are useful in opening up the dialogue between you.

The role of emotions within supervision

Implicit within the supervisory relationship is an awareness and respect for staff's emotional needs. Goleman (1995) described the importance of emotional intelligence for the social life human beings share together. Relationships shape our development. Staff working in early years settings are already familiar with how relationships shape a child's world and are encouraged to use positive relationships with the child to stimulate their development (Department for Education, 2017; Gerhardt, 2004; Sunderland, 2007). Managing behaviours in school settings rely heavily on the relationships that the staff members have between each other and with the students (Dix, 2017).

An understanding of these concepts is helpful and transfers across into supervision. Morrison (2007) described this as the emotional intelligence paradigm. The supervisor is aware of their own emotional responses and able to manage them (intrapersonal relationship). Therefore before supervision the supervisor consciously thinks about their own emotional state and notices how they are feeling. If they become aware that there are feelings aroused by working with this supervisee, the supervisor prepares for this by thinking about why and how they plan to address it. The supervisor takes responsibility for being self-aware and arriving for supervision emotionally regulated. Within the relationship with a supervisee the emotionally intelligent supervisor is alert to how the other person (the supervisee) is feeling and able to use this empathy in managing the relationship between them (interpersonal relationship). This is portrayed in Figure 3.4 below.

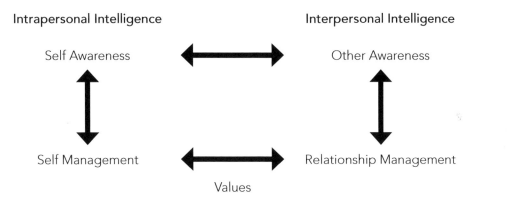

Figure 3.4: The emotional intelligence paradigm. Reprinted with permission by Morrison T (2007). Emotional intelligence, emotion and social work: context, characteristics, complications and contribution. *British Journal of Social Work* **37 245–263.**

Importantly, underpinning the foundations of ethical supervisory practice is an explicit agreement between the participants about the values they share. The Teachers' Standards have clear values that form part of the over-arching principles and these may be referenced in the agreement between each party in the supervision process (Teachers' Standards, 2013 – more detail about using agreements is in Chapter 4).

The art for the supervisor is to facilitate an environment in which the supervisee will best be able to learn. Recognising the emotional state of the supervisee is important in the first instance. Anxiety stimulates the brain into 'doing' mode (fight or flight responses). When students get hyper aroused, staff will be good at soothing and settling them gradually explaining what they are doing or what will be happening, for example 'You will be able to play outside at break time' or using a class distraction technique such as songs or clapping rhythms. It can be tempting sometimes, especially if feeling rushed or under pressure for a supervisor to make a decision, to go straight from seeing to doing and skipping the feeling and thinking stages. This may be likened to a 'quick fix' such as in the example with Mike and the unicycle. The supervisor's skill is to build on this awareness so that they facilitate staff's ability to manage their emotional reactions. Supervisors want staff to think about a range of possible hypotheses rather than only one.

Sometimes this pressure to make decisions quickly, to shift the anxiety, for example abut a child's safety, is hard for supervisors to resist. A very experienced supervisor once explained that she always had 'a cup of tea moment' when she was being pressured by staff into hasty decision making. Taking a breathing space allows the body and emotions a space to calm down and allows time to think through the situation. The experience of making a drink helps the supervisor to prepare emotionally for what they could be dealing with, it gives a supervisee an opportunity to spend a few minutes reviewing what they want to say and, because they feel cared about, increases their ability to self-regulate. Sometimes referred to as 'bottom up/top down' management of an anxiety-inducing state, supervisors will be able to recognise these processes and how to manage staff who have moved into a fight or flight mode of behaving.

This is summarised in Figure 3.5. The three layers are a simplistic design of the doing, feeling and thinking layers of the brain. The doing layer is the brainstem where the rush to action is located often referred to as fight, flight or freeze. Babies are born with this part of their brain the most well developed; able to elicit care by screaming their needs. Gradually, as they are soothed and well cared for, their ability to understand their feelings is facilitated (limbic layer) and they begin to learn language to describe their emotional states and recognise others' emotional states (thinking – cortical layer). Essentially staff in schools are well versed in ensuring students are helped to acquire these skills and to recognise when students are affected by disruptions in their ability to learn. Similar to making a drink, many staff mention how they know the routes around school they can take with dysregulated students, where they are least likely to meet other students, and by the time they have reached a safe space the student's physiological state has calmed sufficiently that they can talk about their distress.

Thinking point

A member of the public with a knife is discovered outside a Year 5 classroom.

■ Scenario 1: rumours spread around the school that a student and member of staff have been attacked.

■ Scenario 2: the head teacher assembles the whole school to debrief about what actually happened and to make sure students feel safe.

Supervision becomes a method for managing the emotional and thinking responses of the staff team.

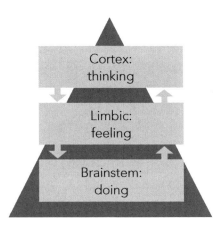

Figure 3.5: Helping staff self-regulate.

The focus of this chapter was to explore how adults learn, and using the learning cycle as its base how the supervision cycle maps onto adults' experience of learning and development. Some of the pitfalls of skipping stages of the learning cycle have been pointed out and the dangers of become too directive as a manager highlighted. The key messages to take away are the art of open questioning and being emotionally attuned as a supervisor. The next chapter focuses on negotiating and fulfilling the role of supervisor, understanding the cornerstones on which supervision is built.

Chapter 4: Putting it all together – the 16 piece integrated model of supervision

Introduction

Essential in making supervision effective in schools are the four cornerstones, the remaining pieces of the 16 piece jigsaw that is the integrated model of supervision. These four elements are:

1. Having a supervision policy.

2. Using working agreements.

3. How supervision sessions are recorded.

4. Formalised reviews.

In this chapter the concept of the authoritative supervisor is introduced, as well as ideas about power and authority that underpin effective authoritative supervisory practice; specifically, the importance of agreeing the terms under which supervision is conducted, the significance of a supervision agreement and the process by which the agreement and subsequent supervisions are recorded. Also included within the chapter are templates to assist these processes. Explicit in a supervision agreement should be the expectation of regular review, including the possibility of an agreement being renegotiated at any point at the request of any party to the agreement. Schools are encouraged to use a supervision policy from which their agreements, recording and review processes flow. There is more detail in Chapter 7 about how the Senior Leadership Team and governing body can use a supervision policy to embed a culture of supervision to make their school compliant with guidelines for safer organisations.

The authoritative supervisor

The authoritative supervisor understands their role, is comfortable with using authority when they need to, and has high expectations of staff, while remaining emotionally attuned to the needs of their supervisee.

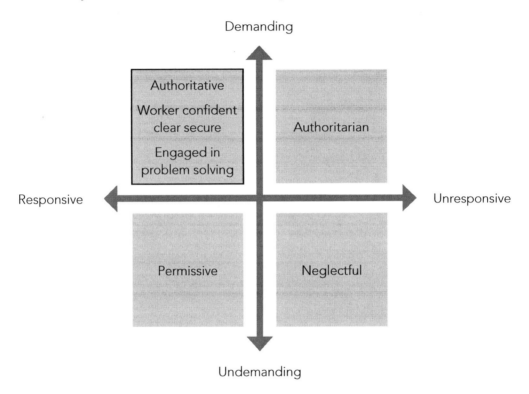

Figure 4.1: The authoritative supervisor. Reprinted with permission from Wonnacott J (2012) *Mastering Social Work Supervision.* **London: Jessica Kingsley Publishers.**

Being an authoritative supervisor requires an understanding of power, as well as being able to use authority. Many forms of power overlap and while they can be used for mutually beneficial purposes, some are very likely to leave open the possibility of misuse. Staff in schools have to be aware of the power they hold relative to students and those governing schools have to be reassured that there are no abuses of power between staff and students, such as have been highlighted in some of the historic cases of sexual and physical abuse currently under greater scrutiny (Erooga, 2018). They also need to know that statutory guidance and codes of conduct are understood and being appropriately followed.

In relation to an understanding of power; supervisors need to be sufficiently self-aware about how they are perceived and the impact their actions may have on others, because of the relative status schools and their staff hold in society, and particularly within their local community.

Thinking point

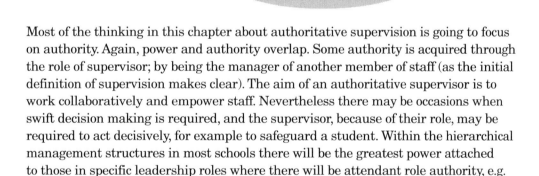

- What does power mean to you?
- How are you affected by any of the following: Gender? Race? Religion? Ability? Age? Class? Culture? Ethnicity? Education? Sexuality? Spirituality?
- Have you faced discrimination because of any of these factors? How did you feel? What happened as a result?
- If you haven't, have you witnessed others being discriminated against? What did you do to challenge their oppression?
- How able do you feel to recognise and support the diverse needs of students, parents and staff?

Most of the thinking in this chapter about authoritative supervision is going to focus on authority. Again, power and authority overlap. Some authority is acquired through the role of supervisor; by being the manager of another member of staff (as the initial definition of supervision makes clear). The aim of an authoritative supervisor is to work collaboratively and empower staff. Nevertheless there may be occasions when swift decision making is required, and the supervisor, because of their role, may be required to act decisively, for example to safeguard a student. Within the hierarchical management structures in most schools there will be the greatest power attached to those in specific leadership roles where there will be attendant role authority, e.g. 'designated safeguarding lead', 'head of year', 'head teacher'.

Other elements of authority combine in the effective supervisor. Supervisors have to be able to understand how they make use of their personal power, using their own assertiveness appropriately and confidently to bring an element of personal authority to their working life. If they are to gain the trust of their supervisees, supervisors need to be viewed as professionals with integrity; this arises from how they use their personal authority in carrying out aspects of their role. Personal authority will be reflected in the moral and ethical judgements that staff make in relation to colleagues and students.

It is also important when working in a professional role that supervisors have comparable professional knowledge to their supervisees to facilitate informed decision making and so they can act using professional authority or, equally importantly, recognise when they have reached the limits of such knowledge. An example of appropriately seeking additional professional knowledge in an authoritative manner might be recognising when the knowledge of an educational psychologist may be required to develop a student's learning because the student has specific learning or emotional needs.

The authoritative supervisor knows the importance of collaboration, of supervisors working to empower their supervisees in the process of engaging effectively in their roles. The supervisor's job is to facilitate a reflective space for staff to bring their knowledge, observations of students and self-awareness, and to challenge, if required, the activities or actions required in order to improve the outcomes for the student(s).

As managers, authoritative supervisors should be clear about the roles and tasks they give their supervisees, ensuring staff have the skills or the opportunity to acquire knowledge. It is also important that the supervisor questions and challenges staff about the quality of their practice, and has high expectations of what they can achieve. Equally they should remain alert to the emotional needs of their supervisees. These important features of authoritative supervision have already been introduced in previous chapters.

Using the ideas outlined here we can begin to form a picture of the ideal authoritative supervisor. Very often staff ideas about 'good' or 'poor' supervisors come from previous experiences of supervision or being managed in other roles.

Thinking point

- Draw/describe your ideal authoritative supervisor.
- What are the most important elements for you?
- What would a new staff member being inducted to your school need from a supervisor?
- How would you go about asking a new staff member about their previous experiences of being managed?

Leading on from this thinking point you may be beginning to recognise that staff may need different things from supervision depending on their individual circumstances. How do effective authoritative supervisors ensure supervision meets the unique needs of each member of staff? The model used in this guide stresses the importance of building relationships between supervisor and supervisee. Supervisors will be assessing supervisee's competence and forming a view about how much direction the supervisee requires. The aim is to increase professional competence. Figure 4.2 summarises the steps on the journey of professional development and increasing the capacity to act autonomously.

Figure 4.2: Adapted with permission from Downey M (2003) *Effective coaching lessons from the coach's coach (2nd Ed)* **London: Cengage Learning.**

Supervisory needs	
Directing ■ Structure. ■ Information. ■ Teaching. ■ Constructive and regular feedback. ■ Encouragement.	**Coaching** ■ Freedom to initiate. ■ Further professional development. ■ To be stretched and challenged. ■ Danger – boredom.
Mentoring ■ Freedom to test out. ■ Space to learn from mistakes. ■ Reflection on realities and constraints.	**Delegating** ■ To be given wider responsibility. ■ To have their experience utilised. ■ Less frequent supervision. ■ Consults with other professionals.

Figure 4.3: Supervisory needs

Effective relationships incorporate trust and respect for each other. Neither of these things are guaranteed to be in place. Trust will be earned by how supervisors and supervisees work together and whether the supervisor does what they have told the supervisee they will. If one party repeatedly alters the arrangement for supervision for example, it will not be possible to build trust up within the relationship as the other person will not feel valued.

Because supervision is a professional conversation, the terms of that conversation should be clarified, including, but not limited to, how disagreements get sorted out. In the pro-forma of a supervision agreement which follows, these points are raised under the section entitled 'making supervision work'. It is also important that how authority is used is clarified. Misuse of power is always unacceptable and codes of conduct and expectations of each other become essential in conveying trust and respect. The model used here sees a supervision agreement as an essential component of effective supervision. Agreeing the terms of supervision is a process that facilitates the development of a relationship within supervision. Before a written agreement is signed a discussion is needed about the elements which are personal to the two people involved and, while there is a template included within this guide, it should never be used prescriptively or in advance of the conversation taking place between a supervisor and a supervisee. The pitfall, especially once supervision becomes audited, is that the supervision agreement becomes a tick box exercise and at its worst filled in by a supervisor without any reference to the supervisee.

There are five steps to establishing an effective working agreement for supervision. The first task is establishing why there is a need for supervision. The feedback in the next chapter (Chapter 5) about what happened when supervision was introduced into five schools and the benefits those participating in it experienced, as well as the links about what makes a safer organisation (in Chapters 6 and 7), may also be relevant at this point.

However, once that is established the method of engaging staff in the process begins. The supervisor may think about how to engage with the staff member as their supervisee, what is required to build a working relationship together, and what each side requires for this to be meaningful to them. This does also need to acknowledge the ambivalence they both may be feeling about being in this position. This is especially likely to be the case during the transition towards a culture of supervision in schools. Many staff will have had years without being expected to receive supervision so to suddenly be encouraged to have it and potentially from a newer member of staff arriving in school might lead to resentment if not managed proactively. There could be tensions around experience and qualification that need to be spoken about before mutual commitment takes place.

The process of writing an agreement, even if a pro-forma is used, will take a few meetings between supervisor and supervisee to enable each party to express their views having had time to think them through. Significantly, for the agreement to be effective it has to be a document that each party knows about and can reference whenever they need to as part of making supervision effective. The agreement has to live up to its descriptor; a process of agreeing how two people or a group decide they are going to work together with shared aims and expectations which they have had the opportunity to discuss with each other and know they can change should they need to. It also becomes part of the record of work.

Developing the supervision agreement

1. Establishing the mandate
2. Engaging with the supervisee
3. Ackknowledging ambivalence
4. The written agreement
5. Reviewing the agreement

> **SUPERVISORY WORKING ALLIANCE**
> The value of a written agreement lies less in the paperwork than in the process by which it has been established

Figure 4.4: Developing the supervisory agreement. Reprinted with permission from Wonnacott J (2014) *Developing and Supporting Staff Supervision Training Pack.* **Brighton: Pavilion Publishing & Media.**

The pro-forma that follows is therefore offered as a guide with the expectation that every supervisor will write a different agreement with each supervisee and that the agreement will be reviewed and changed as the supervisory relationship matures.

Supervision agreement

Agreement between   and

This agreement is designed to be a working tool to underpin the development and maintenance of a good supervisory relationship. The agreement should be:

■ completed at the start of a new supervisory relationship

■ reviewed at least once a year.

The expectations of the provision regarding supervision are set out within the supervision policy, are non-negotiable and provide the framework for this agreement.

The effectiveness of the supervision agreement depends upon the quality of conversation between the supervisor and supervisee, and it is very important that this document provides a foundation for discussion. It should be completed at the conclusion of an exploration of the issues and not become a form filling exercise.

Practical arrangements

Frequency of one-to-one / group supervision.

Duration:

Venue:

Arrangements if either party needs to cancel:

Availability of the supervisor for ad hoc discussions between sessions will be:

Content

The process for agreeing the agenda will be:

Preparation for supervision will include:

Particular priority areas to be discussed regularly:

Making supervision work
What does the supervisee bring to this relationship (e.g. previous work experience, experience of being supervised, preferred learning style)?
What are the supervisee's expectations of the supervisor?
What are the supervisor's expectations of the supervisee?
Are there any factors to acknowledge as relevant to the development of the supervisory relationship (e.g. race, culture, gender, sexual orientation, religious requirements, impairment, including learning difficulties)?
Agreed 'permissions' e.g. it is OK for the supervisor not to know all the answers/for the supervisee to say they are stuck, etc.
How will we recognise when the supervisory relationship is not working effectively?
What methods will be used to resolve any difficulties in working together?
Any other relevant issues for this agreement:
Date agreement due to be reviewed:
Signed:
Supervisor:
Supervisee:
Date:

Thinking point

- How would you introduce this agreement with staff you supervise?
- How would you include the four functions of supervision in this agreement?
- What is missing that you would like to include?

Recording supervision

Schools will have existing systems for recording key information. There are safeguarding children in schools computer programmes which can be particularly beneficial in maintaining a monitoring record related to students caught up in child protection processes. It is not within the scope of this guide to recommend any over another. Schools will need to work out as part of their supervision policy how the key decisions made from supervision are recorded, particularly if they relate to students or staff. Staff employment records should be stored confidentially and staff should be assured that whatever they discuss in supervision is not available to their peers and under what circumstances information from their supervision record may be shared elsewhere, e.g. if there was a capability issue. As part of the agreement there needs to be recognition that supervision records form part of the employee record. Supervisees should be given a copy of what has been recorded about them from supervision, be encouraged to read it and bring back to their supervisor where they may feel the recording is an inaccurate account of their discussion.

Similarly where there are child protection concerns or issues about a student's learning, then the school has to have clear, confidential arrangements for the storage of those records and part of the decision making in the supervisory meeting should include how and when the information will be shared with the parent(s) of the student as well as the student themselves. What needs to be recorded where and when will need to link to the supervisory policy so staff and supervisors are clear about recording.

Also of note here is the finding in a summary of Serious Case Reviews conducted after staff had abused children in school settings, that concerns which were building up about behaviour of staff were voiced but not systematically recorded so that a picture of 'accumulating concern' could emerge (Wonnacott, 2018).

Thinking point

- A parent rings your school raising concerns that their child has reported a member of staff touching them during an after school games activity.

- How confident would you be in your school that the parent's concerns for their child were appropriately investigated and recorded?

Included here are ideas about a structure for recording supervision; they give a framework that could be used as an agenda. However effective supervision relies on the negotiation between two people and their ability to trust one another in carrying out the tasks expected of their roles. Therefore any pro-forma is flexible and should be seen as a tool to be adapted.

Sample student record sheet

Student:	
Supervisee:	Supervisor:
Date:	

Agenda item	Summary of discussion	Decisions/ actions	Responsible person	Timescale
Experience/ information discussed				
Reflections (feelings)				
Analysis (how understanding of the issues was reached)				
Action plan				
Signed: supervisor	Date	Copy on student's record		
Signature: supervisee	Date			

Sample supervision record

Supervision record	
Supervisee:	Supervisor:
Date:	

Agenda item	Summary of discussion	Decisions/ actions	Responsible person	Timescale
Issues relating to staff development. E.g. feedback from training. Progress in respect of the professional development plan (PDP). Development opportunities.				
Issues relating to staff support E.g. sickness. Any current stressors or issues relating to staff well-being (including workload review). Reasonable adjustments under Disability Discrimination Act if required.				
Issues relating to professional practice and school requirements. E.g. impact of any new policies/ procedures/organisational expectations. Consideration of what has worked well in relation to practice. Any issues relating to quality of practice/performance.				
Any other issues				
Signed: supervisor	Date	A copy to be given to supervisee and a copy retained and filed securely by the supervisor.		
Signature: supervisee	Date			

Thinking point

- What is currently working well in your school recording systems for students/staff members?
- What could be improved?

Using the concept of a learning journey helps to explain the purpose of the separate processes of recording. Supervision records should show 'the working out' of why decisions about students and staff are made. Historically public organisations have been criticised for not explaining *why* they do what they do. This lack of transparency has promoted a sense of secrecy and exclusion, often unintentionally. The test that is useful in identifying what needs to be recorded is; 'If I were a stranger picking up these records, would I understand why the decisions were made? Can I follow how this student made progress and "journeyed" through the school?' They also contribute useful evidence to reviews of practice and assist others in learning how progress and change in student's learning ability is brought about.

For staff, a record of discussions held in supervision or supervisory group meetings may provide good evidence that can add to evaluations of their practice and professional development that form part of their appraisals. Supervision records form part of the review of the supervisory process that is a necessary part of effective supervision.

The authoritative supervisor builds relationships with supervisees which take account of power and authority and understands how they may be used or abused in supervision. The authoritative supervisor uses their emotional intelligence effectively in their relationships with staff. The concept of authoritative supervisory practice has offered a structure in this chapter to introduce the importance of developing a working agreement between supervisor and supervisee. The agreement needs to be more than a document that is filed away for an audit process as it is a key tool in making an effective supervisory relationship. Accurate recording has also been highlighted as it tells the story of how students and staff develop in their respective learning journeys. This chapter concludes the core components of supervision, the 16 pieces making up the integrated model of supervision.

The next chapter discusses using this model in a range of schools. It details how this method of supervision was applied to the everyday experiences of school settings.

Chapter 5: Supervision in practice – the role of the Designated Safeguarding Lead

Introduction

This chapter is based on the outcomes of piloting of the supervision model in schools and which focuses on the role of the Designated Safeguarding Lead (DSL). Over the academic year 2016-2017 a pilot trialling supervision in schools was conducted in five schools in two neighbouring local authorities.

The pilot involved a secondary school with pupils from Year 7 to Year 13, one special school with pupils from Reception to Year 11, a first school with pupils from Reception to Year 4, and two primary schools with pupils from Reception to Year 6, one of which was two separate schools; infant and junior. This provided a unique opportunity to find out how the model could be adapted to each setting.

In this chapter the following terms are used:

- DSL for Designated Safeguarding Lead.
- DDSL for Deputy Designated Safeguarding Lead.
- The DSL or DDSL led supervision in their own school setting.
- Teachers and Teaching Assistants working in schools with children and young people received supervision from their DSL or DDSL.

What the pilot offered

The pilot offered to work with participating schools to find effective methods of establishing supervision in school settings. The impetus for this pilot came from those working in the DSL role who felt challenged by cuts to other provisions, aware of children with unmet needs in school and the associated emotional burden on staff.

Each school had received training and guidance prior to enrolment in the pilot.

Schools participating in this pilot received support from the authors who worked with them to develop an approach to supervision in line with both national expectations and established good safeguarding practice. This allowed schools to tailor their own supervisory systems in their schools with their staff teams to meet their individual needs. Each school had a school-based meeting every term, usually, but not exclusively, an individual consultation with one of the authors.

Those schools participating in the process were encouraged to join a community of practice, learning from others and working together towards finding solutions to any challenges arising.

A representative from each school (usually the Designated Safeguarding Lead, or the Deputy Designated Safeguarding Lead) attended a termly group supervision meeting led by the authors. These meetings enabled DSLs to consider their role in school, discuss safeguarding concerns, and use the experience of the group to develop their knowledge and skills. The DSLs decided how they would develop supervision within their own schools. One DSL saw every member of staff once a fortnight for ten minutes to focus on concerns. Another DSL saw a class team every term for a group supervision session. Each school used the time they felt they had available and used a structure with a clear focus to discuss safeguarding concerns.

To establish an evidence base of what is effective within a school environment, questionnaires were completed at the beginning and end of the pilot, by both the DSLs/DDSLs and staff teams that they supervised.

Before the pilot began, one DSL stated their best hopes about facilitating regular supervision in the school to be:

> *'The staff will feel better equipped to support the needs of pupils in their care. That they will be better informed to work with families and meet the needs of pupils. That these will be a positive impact on the pupils' engagement with education and attainment.'*

Supervision in schools pilot findings

It is useful to consider the findings of the pilot under the headings of the four functions of supervision: emotional support, professional development, management and mediation.

Support function

The importance of emotional support

Three distinct areas emerged with regard to the importance of emotional support. Firstly, the benefit to staff in schools of having their emotional needs recognised. Secondly, an awareness that the pilot legitimised a need for emotional support in the role of DSL and how to sustain that support after the pilot. And thirdly, the impact of being the worker at the boundary between the school and social care resulting in knowing more about what students' lives are like outside school. One DSL stated that:

> *'Emotionally it is an exhausting and exhilarating job in equal measure. There are a huge range of emotions that are experienced on a daily basis. By being able to begin to order and work through these emotions through supervision has benefitted my practice.'*

In offering supervision to staff they were given space to feel. This was welcomed and assisted with managing the emotionally demanding aspects of both the teaching role as well as the safeguarding elements within schools. In particular, dealing with and responding to those students who need to be safeguarded before they are ready to learn and whose behaviour can interfere with other students' learning. One DSL commented at the end of the pilot that:

> *'The role can be emotionally draining and sometimes you do not always recognise this impact. Supervision gives you the time, space and permission to acknowledge and explore this, to ensure we are giving children our best in terms of safeguarding.'*

The feedback from schools included a recognition that offering staff regular supervision gave them a space to offload; it offered the chance to take notice of how staff are feeling about students and ask questions about why; and it helped staff to recognise when they need to take steps to look after themselves, including when to seek support from others, whether that is within the school or outside it. One teacher stated that supervision '… *builds resilience and energy to cope*'. All five DSL supervisors rated '*having resilience – the ability to keep going under stress*' as very important.

Participants in the pilot felt that this legitimised a need for emotional support in the DSL role. This has given rise to questions about what to do if there is limited emotional support available within the school for the DSL or within the existing networks and how will this be provided after the pilot? One DSL wrote at the end of the pilot:

'I believe myself to be fairly experienced in the field of safeguarding and child protection and in being able to meet the needs of my teachers and class teams... I have found it beneficial to receive supervision [from the consultant] *in my own role, to consider my needs, and to have the chance to talk through some difficult cases.'*

In some schools being part of a bigger trust offers opportunities for support across networks of schools and in some, Governors are available who are highly skilled. However, this is dependent on having the 'right' people rather than roles and expectations of practice within schools.

DSLs have also highlighted the emotional impact of being the school representative at social care meetings and being privy to information about students which can be highly distressing. They also must manage the consequences of social care decision making, e.g. when students move placements, necessitating a change of school and helping the students in those transitions. This is a significant part of the role of the DSL and has emotional consequences for staff. Finding strategies to manage these demands will need to be determined in each school. There are emotional consequences and finding satisfactory solutions when these situations feel overwhelming kept emerging as a discussion point. The supervision provided during the pilot highlighted that:

'In a very student centred establishment it has allowed me to begin to understand and focus on the impact safeguarding has on staff.'

Staff reported they felt cared for by having regular timetabled supervision. One head teacher, the DSL, commented about the group supervision received from the authors:

'It is at times a very isolated role and supervision has helped me to feel supported.'

There are several areas of interest to the authors regarding the positive impact of supervision on staff sickness and the impact of staff supervision on students' educational outcomes that were beyond the scope of this project. However, at the end of the project one DSL stated that one impact that supervision had on the safeguarding role was:

'Greater awareness of the impact of staff emotional needs impacting on pupils day to day.'

Professional development function

Development of skills and knowledge

All the DSLs and all of the staff that they supervised felt that their own knowledge and skills had developed as a result of supervision. The knowledge and skills that were listed by the DSLs were:

- *'Knowledge about how social care work.'*
- *'Procedures and practices for safeguarding.'*
- *'Ability to question assumptions and practices.'*
- *'Good information sharing.'*
- *'Use of other tools/opinions to support actions.'*
- *'Being guided to facilitate supervision.'*
- *'Greater awareness of the strategies I use to cope.'*
- *'Improved resilience.'*
- *'Greater understanding of the impact of supervision.'*
- *'Listening and coaching skills developed.'*

The knowledge and skills identified by the staff the DSL's supervised were:

- *'Ways of handling difficult situations with parents.'*
- *'Reflection and resilience.'*
- *'Better understanding of behaviour triggers and how to respond to them.'*
- *'Understanding the impact on me.'*
- *'Improved reflection and ability to support colleagues.'*
- *'Reflection skills.'*
- *'Specifics on external agencies and ability to refer. Ability to lead meetings effectively.'*
- *'Time management.'*

The DSLs were asked to try to identify how their skills and that of their staff had developed. The following were identified by the DSLs:

- *'By talking through and discussing.'*
- *'Sharing ideas.'*
- *'Being willing to escalate.'*
- *'Becoming aware of profiling tools that can identify level of need.'*

- *'My own ability to facilitate staff to reflect upon how they acted and how they can improve their practice has improved.'*
- *'By reflecting, questioning, clarifying and summarising.'*
- *'By using listening skills to allow staff to begin to solve concerns and problems themselves.'*
- *'Understanding how to prioritise job responsibilities on a daily basis.'*

And for the staff that were supervised this developed by:
- *'Able to reflect on a previous case and discuss how things would be dealt with differently next time.'*
- *'Working with supervisor.'*
- *'Reflection and questioning, supervision, and conversations with colleagues.'*
- *'Having time to reflect and discuss. Conversations with colleagues.'*
- *'Time to think. Being challenged. Questioning.'*
- *'Through discussion and collaborative planning.'*
- *'Understanding how to prioritise job responsibilities on a daily basis.'*

The development of knowledge and skills was seen by all to be a direct result of the regularly scheduled supervision. They felt this new level of knowledge and skills to be 'good development' in the post-pilot questionnaire.

Increased confidence around safeguarding role

The increase in staff awareness of safeguarding and their development of skills and knowledge during the pilot had a direct, positive impact on staff confidence about their role and relationships with each other, with other professionals and with students and parents (the people/ stakeholders who benefit from supervision). Supervision provided a space to challenge assumptions and to think through what the next steps could/should be. One teacher stated:

> *'Supervision has given me confidence in my ability to make judgements and decisions.'*

Importance of preparation

As supervision was a planned activity, both parties, DSL and the staff they supervised, made sure they prepared for the meetings. It allowed for a shared agenda and prior thinking about what they wanted to achieve, which made the meetings purposeful. At the end of the pilot one DSL wrote:

'It allowed me to not only ensure staff had the opportunity to disclose or discuss issues but it also allowed me time to plan for any issues I needed to raise with them.'

Preparation for supervision was identified as an important part of the process as staff: *'... already knew the case and had already started to reflect on it.'*

Identification of training needs

Supervision was seen by school staff as an opportunity to identify training needs. One teaching assistant wrote before the pilot that they hoped:

'To gain help and support in areas where I have little or no experience; to identify training needs and share best practice.'

By offering emotional care and support it was possible to identify opportunities for professional development and empower staff in cascading training to others, for example recognising neglect. Supervision allowed staff: *'to share best practice and support staff development.'*

Management function

Clarification of safeguarding roles

As a result of receiving supervision, staff reported they understood their roles in safeguarding students better. In one school the process of supervision had: *'... caused me to consider the processes and practices in our school.'*

Another school used the supervision process to build a new safeguarding team which improved relationships within the school with other staff members.

Schools also reported that there had been a change in how they recorded and shared information. One DSL stated the importance of all school staff:

'... understanding support systems in place to protect, safeguard and support children and families.'

Improved information gathering

It was hoped that regular supervision will result in:

'...more information about young people being shared to provide a better picture of all young people in the school.'

There was a noticeable increase in reporting low level concerns. Information gathering improved and staff ability to think, to analyse information and to problem solve improved too. One DSL noticed:

'Identifying areas of concern and allowing staff to begin to solve cases and problems for themselves [increased during the pilot].'

One school recognised that although they used an:

'… electronic recording system for safeguarding concerns and whilst this is effective, providing face-to-face supervision enables the transfer of much more than just the facts. Staff are encouraged to use their "gut feeling" around their concerns and a clearer explanation of this was possible through direct conversations.'

Time

How time is prioritised effectively is an on-going challenge within schools. One teaching assistant wrote about the job being *'intense and fast paced.'* But hoped that:

'…supervision will help as it will give me time to actually reflect and be given support on what things may be able to be done differently.'

Before the start of the pilot, all of the DSLs identified having enough time to do supervision to be a concern. For example, one DSL wrote, *'Time will be a limiting factor if not handled correctly.'*

Another stated their concern around having *'…time to conduct meaningful supervision.'*

This concern was overcome by making a commitment to timetabling supervision into the school timetable at the beginning of the academic year. Supervision was timetabled in and staff were expected to adhere to it, which meant they turned up ready to use the time. One DSL commented on the importance of:

'…identifying diary time in advance and keeping it sacred when so many things crop up.'

Once staff understood the functions of supervision, they made it a priority and used it well.

The DSL role tends to be a reactive role and one of the questions the DSLs asked was what would change by having more regular meetings (supervision) with staff? One supervisee identified the impact of supervision to have made the safeguarding role '...*more thoughtful, less knee-jerk.*'

The DSLs had arranged to meet key staff regularly and shared an expectation that staff planned and prepared for supervision. In one school the head teacher sent:

> '...*emails to identify areas to discuss so are prepared and therefore time usefully spent.....Knew case and had already reflected on it. So agenda known in advance.*'

The desired outcome was that this would build staff awareness and flexibility of response to lessen the opportunities for crises occurring. The consensus throughout was that they were building a culture of reflecting and thinking about what is happening rather than only reacting to what is or has happened. For example, the DSLs reported giving themselves permission to take the time to think before supervision sessions, as they needed to prepare for supervision with staff too. By doing this, probable consequences of the decisions or plans made could be thought through in advance.

The working hypothesis for the pilot was that planned meetings (supervision) might mean more effective management and support of the more vulnerable or at risk students by offering emotional support to staff working with them. One DSL wrote that her best hopes about facilitating regular supervision was that:

> '*Improved practice will lead to better and more timely outcomes for children and families.*'

After the pilot ended one DSL noted that:

> '*I believe that supervision enabled better understanding and consideration of home circumstances, previous history, current obstacles to parenting. This enabled staff to offer better support for pupils from a more informed position.*'

Each school, despite the challenges of context and time, made a commitment to change. At each school the DSL with their selected staff was proactive. Each DSL decided to whom they offered supervision either individually or in groups. Gradually the expectations became clearer about what could and should be discussed. There were fruitful discussions within the schools and amongst the combined group thinking about who on the staff team needs to know what information to effectively safeguard students, including sharing computer systems which facilitated this.

Earlier discussion of concerns

The DSLs had noted that staff shared their concerns about students earlier. For example, in one school:

> 'Regularly checking with staff to ensure the opportunity was given for them to be able to express concerns before they got too big.'

Supervision gave them an opportunity to have regular updates about what had happened to information they had shared previously and likely consequences, for example the social care thresholds were better understood.

Mediation function

Importance of commitment from senior leadership team

In reviewing why the pilot had worked as well as it did, it was acknowledged that there had been commitment from the Senior Leadership Team (SLT). The staff who offered supervision had made a commitment to it and prioritised time for it. This included preparation and understanding the aims of supervision. In one school the DSL identified that:

> 'There is a need for greater understanding amongst all SLT of the importance of the supervision process.'

Conclusions

The Integrated Model of Supervision has been seen to work well in schools once the purpose of each element was understood and used. It was flexible enough to be adapted to meet each school's needs. For example, in the pilot some schools used supervision as a group intervention working with class teams, some used it individually supporting the pastoral leaders, others used it to develop a safeguarding team. At the end of the pilot one DSL wrote:

> 'From the discussions we have held as a group of participating schools, it has been useful to consider others' approaches, although it is very apparent that each setting needs to find what works best for them.'

Schools are beginning to be much more aware of the role and scope of supervision for their staff teams. One teacher wrote at the end of the pilot:

'I was not really aware prior to the project of what regular supervision might be, but feel that it has been really beneficial and supportive.'

The schools taking part in the project identified the impact that supervision had on the safeguarding role as being diverse. This included the impact of supervision for the DSL:

'It gave me time to talk about things that were bothering me. It also gave me time to talk to a skilled person about things I did not know or had never come across before.'

The impact of providing supervision for school staff members:

'It enabled me to recognise and meet the needs of my staff and ensure well-being was considered for all.'

And the impact of supervision for staff on students:

'It gave me time to reflect on the role that I have and to consider the best way to support the pupil's current needs, and ensuring I regularly reflect and adapt my responses to the pupil's needs.'

School staff felt that supervision developed their knowledge and skills which had a positive impact on their confidence. It also gave them time to think and discuss the students in their care, and:

'… allowed me to reflect on good practice and on things I could improve.'

Supervision was regarded as positive and beneficial by all of the members of staff involved in the pilot.

Chapter 6: Putting supervision into practice in schools

Introduction

Now that all 16 pieces of the jigsaw have been explained, and the model in its entirety assembled, there may well be questions about how to implement it effectively in your school. This chapter offers some ideas, drawing on a range of sources, about how supervision becomes a major component in supporting staff and developing their resilience to dealing with stressful situations. Effective supervision starts with effective supervisors.

Stress busting supervision

One of the supervisors in the pilot offered his pastoral leads a ten minute individual supervision every other week, in addition to the already existing weekly management group meeting with them all. His opening question was 'How are you?'. One day one of the pastoral leads was struggling with the competing demands of her workload. Because she knew he cared, she asked for help on a crisis basis and they reprioritised her workload.

The supervisor was surprised. Firstly, because it had not been obvious to him how stressed his colleague had become, and this therefore indicated to him how much stress was being hidden from the senior leadership team, and secondly, that making sure he spared ten minutes a fortnight for a colleague, translated into 'he cares' better than anything from his previous management style had.

Finding an hour every term for each member of staff transformed the relationships within the pastoral team. The people involved in this scenario were convinced that without supervision the pastoral lead would have gone off sick. Let's be clear, supervision was a scheduled meeting with an agreement and clarity about how it dovetailed with the other expectations of the (16 piece) integrated model. It can be hard in the pressured environments of schools to justify taking and using time for supervision which is why this example is included. The supervisor needed to find something he could commit to, and sparing 30 minutes a week to see the six members of his pastoral team individually in the course of a fortnight felt manageable. Alleviating the crisis and facilitating his colleague with her work, resulted in her being able to stay at work and effectively manage her workload rather than going off sick and adding to the pressures of others within the school.

This seems important in the current context when there are headlines such as *'Epidemic of stress' blamed for 3,750 teachers on long term sick leave'* (Asthana & Boycott-Owen, 2018). This is attributed to the pressures of work, anxiety and rising levels of mental illness. Supervision is one method for checking in (but not checking up on) to make sure that staff are managing their workload and offering them support to do so. It makes explicit that supervisors care rather than relying on assumptions that they do.

Thinking point

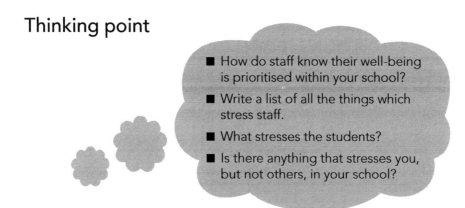

- How do staff know their well-being is prioritised within your school?
- Write a list of all the things which stress staff.
- What stresses the students?
- Is there anything that stresses you, but not others, in your school?

The emotionally intelligent supervisor

Chapter 3 touched on the importance of managing the emotional needs of supervisor and supervisee for supervision to be effective. The concepts of emotional intelligence were introduced in thinking about how important it was that the supervisor took responsibility for being prepared for supervision and beginning it in a calm, thoughtful and self-aware state. Dix's (2017) five pillars for good school behaviour management begin with consistent, calm, adult behaviour. This is essentially the starting point of effective supervision.

There are many pressures on school staff. The workload pressures lead to teachers working longer hours, which brings knock on effects to having a work/life balance especially for those with parenting or caring responsibilities too. They can feel as if they are not 'up to the job' if they raise issues about their own needs.

Staff with additional safeguarding or pastoral responsibilities may be exposed to information about students and what happens in their home lives which others in the school do not know. Sometimes they will attend meetings and hear information about the students they know, other children in the family or the family's circumstances, that are shocking. Many DSLs speak about the distressing impact attending a child protection case conference for the first time had on them and how unprepared they felt for what they would be confronted with.

There are fewer agencies outside schools available to help students who have additional emotional needs which interfere with their ability to learn. The students themselves may be traumatised and their behaviour may be difficult to manage or contain in school settings.

Traumatised students may have a big impact on the adults in their environment as they push against the school's boundaries (Bombèr & Hughes 2013; Dix, 2017). Finding methods to help staff deal with how they feel about what they have heard, seen or in other ways had to deal with, may at times be acutely necessary.

> *'I became more aware of how I had found coping with physical assaults and I needed time to discuss this and isolate my emotions in order to continue working with the pupil.'* (supervisee in the pilot)

The awareness that members of staff could be affected by secondary trauma, also known as vicarious trauma or compassion fatigue, may need highlighting within the senior leadership teams and can be identified through supervision.

Additional pressures from the current climate in teaching are that it is always possible to be in contact with school and its demands; turning off requires self-discipline. Emails can always be checked and responded to. School staff are working outside the school building by remaining connected through technology. Cultures can build up within schools about expectations of responsiveness to emails, which may be being sent at weekends or during the evening.

Staff in leadership roles, and especially when they take on the responsibilities of supervising others, need to think about the impact of their behaviour on those they manage. Head teachers may find it helpful to deal with emails before the working day or late at night, but what impact does receiving an email at that time have on the head of year trying to deal with her own family needs. In Chapter 4 this was discussed in the context of consciously being aware of how supervisors use their own personal and professional power authoritatively. This chapter builds on that self-awareness and its impact on others.

Thinking point

- Review the last week. How much time did you spend on the following activities?
  - Focused on an intellectually stimulating activity.
  - Spending time with close family, friends, your natural environment.
  - Spontaneous 'play/creative' time.
  - Chill time – no activity or focus.
  - Reflective space to review your thoughts and feelings.
  - Sleeping.
  - Being physically active.

These are the essential components of a healthy mind (Rock & Siegel, 2012). How healthy is your mind? Congratulate yourself for things you are doing well each week.

- What are you resolved to do more of?

Emotionally intelligent school leadership

An emotionally intelligent leader is reflective, aware of their impact on others, able to read the emotional cues of other people, whether they are adults or students, and is attuned to the emotional needs of the group.

A teacher friend commented that when she began teaching she had assumed her specialist subject knowledge was the key part of her skillset, decades later she knows that it is how well she manages, reads and understands students' behaviour. Goleman (1995) was the first to identify and explain what emotional intelligence was and his interest has spawned an industry in exploring what happens in human groups. Schools will be working with students across the range of their development from Early Years Foundation Stage up to their entry into further and higher education, apprenticeships or employment. School staff will usually be the first people who are not parental figures to offer models of authoritative, respectful use of power. It is therefore essential that there are emotionally intelligent school leaders from Early Years to the end of secondary education.

Figure 6.1 describes how behaviour spirals once it gets caught in a cycle. The red cycle will be triggered by different emotions for different people. There will be numerous occasions when you have witnessed 'red behaviour' from students, parents and staff. Change often provokes red behaviour by asking staff to do things they feel unconfident about, which increases their anxiety. If there is no space to reflect on the uncertainties and to ask questions, the red behaviour is promoted, leading to defensiveness, denial or withdrawal (that may present as things like staff turnover, sickness, a chaotic school environment). The red cycle behaviour is a compromised behavioural response to anxiety/uncertainty and when it features in organisations can be hugely disruptive to the purpose of the organisation. It is not a personality trait but how anyone under pressure may find themselves reacting if they are not helped into a more reflective stance.

Contrast that with the uncertainty, risk taking and creativity that is part of a 'green' behaviour pattern. The starting point of an anxiety-provoking situation may look similar but it is responded to differently.

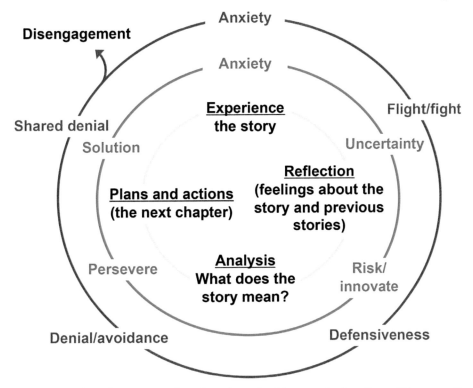

Figure 6.1: Red and green cycles. Reprinted with permission from Wonnacott J (2014) *Developing and Supporting Effective Staff Supervision*. Pavilion Publishing and Media.

Thinking point

■ Think back over a time when you witnessed red behaviour. What did you see? How did you feel? Who had the power in the situation and what happened as a consequence?

■ Have you witnessed two adults in school displaying red behaviour? What happened?

Red behaviour is powerful. Adults caught up in red behaviour have lost their ability to manage themselves in a professional manner. The purpose of red behaviour is to stop thinking, and the pressured speech that often results makes thinking particularly difficult. There may well be other physical signs of agitation. Imagine two scenarios of a plane hitting turbulence. In one, the steward running up and down a plane saying 'we're all going to die' will engender panic. Passengers expect the professionals to remain calm and will be increasingly fearful if staff are not. Whereas in scenario two the pilot in the leadership role remaining calm, advising safe action to take may well be facing uncertainty but will keep the crew and passengers calm. 'Think green' is a good mantra for leadership in high pressure environments especially when there is a real chance of behaviour contagion.

Thinking green is about staying emotionally aware, alert to personal signs of stress and aware of it surfacing in others, and looking for ways to alleviate those pressures. The ability to develop a flexible mindset is a useful strategy in effective supervision as well as a buffer against stress. It is a factor in remaining resilient in the face of constant change.

A flexible mindset – developing good coping skills

The chart overleaf uses the psychological concepts around coping to help staff identify their preferred strategies and review whether there are others they can adopt. The column on the left is a descriptor of behaviours which could describe responses to stressful situations. The blank column on the right is for you or your staff members to pay attention to how you respond.

General coping style	My coping style – do I do these always, sometimes, never?
Active coping; *taking your own actions, initiatives*	
Planning; *anticipating, thinking through scenarios, working out strategies*	
Seeking social support; *advice/information gathering*	
Seeking emotional social support	
Suppressing competing activities; *avoiding getting distracted and being able to focus*	
Spiritual support; *identifying and using religious/spiritual support*	
Positive reinterpretation and growth; *able to reframe a situation into a more positive light*	
Restraint; *able to identify and wait for the right time to act*	
Resignation/acceptance; *accepting a challenging situation*	
Focusing on and venting emotion	
Denial; *refusing to accept a problem exists*	
Mental disengagement; *using distraction to stop thinking about the issues*	
Behavioural disengagement; *doing other things to avoid the issues*	
Alcohol/drug/food use; *using food, drink or tablets to avoid the situation or as self-medication*	
Humour	

(Based on the work of Carver (1989) quoted in Grant & Kinman (2014) and developed by the authors.)

Having filled this in you will be aware that there are no 'right' or 'wrong' answers. All of us at times use any, indeed many, of these methods. This chart is designed to help you to challenge yourself towards more functional coping methods. For example, if after work you only want chocolate and/or a drink of alcohol rather than ever feeling tempted to be sociable or exercise.

Safe space

Supervision has to be conducted in safe, confidential spaces, preferably in rooms where it can be carried out uninterrupted. Staff need to feel comfortable in supervision.

Susan Cain (2011) writes about the need for 'sane spaces' and 'restorative niches'. She describes research about the impact of working in open plan offices as reducing productivity, impairing memory, leading to high staff turnover by making people sick, hostile, unmotivated and insecure. Staff are more likely to suffer from high blood pressure, have elevated stress levels and get the flu. There are more arguments between colleagues. It seems that this is attributable to the rising levels of cortisol (the stress hormone). This activates the fight or flight responses leading us to become emotionally distant, quicker to anger and less available to help others ('red behaviour'). There has been a noticeable decrease in spaces available to staff to be quiet in and the pressure within schools on room makes finding the 'sane space' or 'restorative niche' challenging. In our highly connected world, especially in environments where all spaces have multiple occupants in them, where are the 'sane' spaces to reflect on what has just happened, whether for staff or students?

'Being in a role where a pupil regularly offers abuse, both emotional and physical, is emotionally hard to manage. It is hard to stay positive about the pupil at times, but have learnt the need to share the emotion I feel in a different way so other staff are not overhearing.' (Teaching assistant from pilot reflecting on the benefits of supervision.)

Negotiating a safe, uninterrupted space was an important learning point from the pilot. To begin with, supervision took place in shared offices or rooms where others had access. Gradually as staff valued the process more and more, they understood how essential having a space in which they could think, where others would not interrupt and where confidentiality could be maintained, was to making supervision effective. Even the head teachers or DSLs who operated open door policies learnt the value for themselves of saying that some meetings could not be interrupted. Protecting space prioritises and promotes a school culture that facilitates supervision and perceives the benefits to staff and students of doing it well.

If someone knows they need time by themselves to replenish their energy (introverted personality type) how can they carve out the restorative space they need? We all need strategies to protect and value our thinking time.

Identifying quiet spaces will assist students as well as staff. It is helpful to have a range of techniques known and used within schools to recognise and deal with behaviour that stems from an activation of trauma. Using trauma-informed approaches will assist all students in learning. Supervision may be a place to gather ideas and find out what has worked with particular students or to discuss what has become known about what triggers certain behaviours.

The first part of this chapter has emphasised the importance of self-management, emotional intelligence and remaining calm when in senior leadership or supervisory roles. Effective supervisors also facilitate supervisees getting the most out of supervision.

Strategies to help supervisees

An agreement negotiated by both parties about how they will work together using supervision is the best preparation for making supervision effective. Chapter 4 included a template for an agreement between supervisor and supervisee. Through the process of negotiating an agreement, the purpose of supervision is explored, the consequences of 'what happens if' can be talked about so that they are known. This should definitely include what can be kept confidential and what cannot be kept confidential. It should also include how to review the agreement incorporating who will be approached if there are difficulties between supervisor and supervisee which they cannot resolve themselves.

From the pilot, different schools found different methods worked for them when preparing for supervision. Some liked an agenda that was negotiated on email in advance, others decided at the previous meeting what topics would be covered, others decided when they arrived. Supervisees need to feel that supervision is 'their meeting' and should feel able to contribute to the agenda and what gets discussed, although it is also a space for supervisors to give feedback and ensure that management accountabilities are being pursued too. It may be helpful to refer back to the discussion in Chapter 1 about the boundaries between performance appraisal and supervision.

When supervision is effective, the supervisor models the sharing of power and responsibility to encourage the supervisee's professional development. So, in similar ways to how students are encouraged to mentor and give feedback to one another, it is useful if supervisees arrive thinking about work they are proud of, and that has gone well, to ensure that what they are doing well is noted and feedback sought on it. It also helps to come prepared to discuss something they wish to improve, or where something unexpected happened. Only focusing on problems becomes disempowering and it is crucial that staff are encouraged to look for situations they are doing well to build their professional confidence, especially in the early stages of a new job role. From work conducted with other professions there are benefits to keeping a reflective journal noting how staff feel about their professional life (Grant & Kinman, 2014). Keeping a journal tracking emotional responses to daily life is a known factor in maintaining resilience and develops the self-reflective skills of emotional intelligence.

Thinking point

- Think back about a crisis in your career when you considered leaving teaching.
  - Why did you want to leave?
  - What made you decide to stay?
  - What would you tell your younger self now?

Group supervision

Because of the collective nature of schools and the naturally occurring groups of staff, some schools in the pilot ran group supervision. The obvious ones were either when there was a group of staff working together in the same class because there were several, or all, students with additional needs, or where there was a shared focus, for example the pastoral or safeguarding team. Again a negotiated agreement is immensely important, differentiating between supervision and other meetings with the same people in it that have a different focus, e.g. lesson planning. In some schools there was both individual supervision and group supervision and a clearly negotiated agreement is necessary about what is discussed where. For example, with the supervisor offering ten minute fortnightly individual supervision the focus of this was emotional support, and the weekly group meeting included the other functions of supervision; management, mediation and professional development. In other schools, supervision was offered to and for a group with a shared purpose, so either working with a particular unchanging group of students in a class setting or as a safeguarding team. Clarifying the boundaries and responsibilities of group members was seen as an important learning point, also having a structure to reflect and participate in how they responded to students enhanced staff confidence. As with individual supervision, having space which encouraged staff to explore how they were feeling and especially how they felt in relation to the issues arising with the students, particularly those caught up in child protection processes, was really valued.

Proposed agenda for group supervision (based on the supervision cycle)

Task	Function	Outcome
Introduction	Clarifying roles and confidentiality.	Agreed expectations.
Experience	Sharing experiences, what is working well and who would welcome space to explore further.	Agenda making – which issues have priority and who has reflective space today (up to 3 x 20 minute discussions?).
Reflection	How protagonist feels, who else is affected and how are they feeling? Different levels of reflection. Opportunity to check what assumptions have been made?	Assessment of impact.
Analysis	What understanding of the issue can be reached? Which theories/policies or procedures assist with making sense of the experiences?	A range of options and meanings explored with likely consequences considered.
Action planning	What needs to happen next? Who should do it and what support/training is needed?	Decision making and responsibility assigned.
Review of group process	Assessing impact for others of discussion and supporting in meeting emotional needs.	Concluding group with summary of learning and what actions required by whom with timescales agreed and summary recorded.

The effective part of supervision is to remember it is a learning and development tool to assist staff in their professional development. Effective supervision is the ability to ask questions which generate new ways of thinking for staff (Chapter 3). Managing the emotional responses, the information that is being generated and helping to stimulate supervisee's professional development by getting them to analyse and reach their own solution can be overwhelming. This is particularly the case when working with groups of staff or in situations about which there is an increasing level of anxiety. The supervisor may find themselves facing 'red behaviour' and needing to remember to 'think green'. A useful tool to use in such situations is the 'discrepancy matrix'. It is called this as there will often be pieces of information which do not fit together, that are unclear, or that are missing, and that are part of the issue which needs analysing. Using the matrix organises the information and challenges assumptions that might be impeding staff responses.

The best way of becoming convinced about the usefulness of this tool is to try it out, however a scenario is provided to show it being applied in a school context.

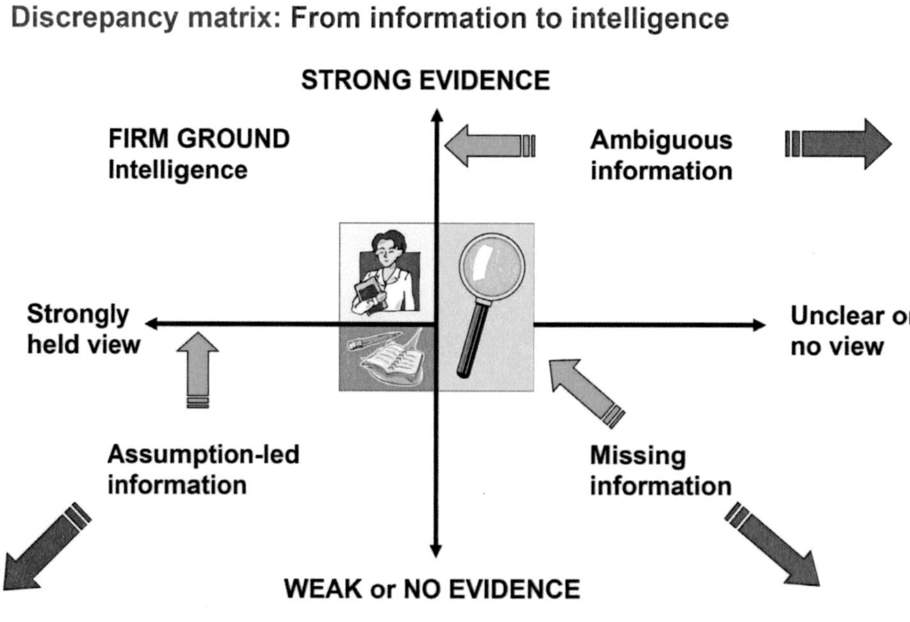

Discrepancy matrix: From information to intelligence

STRONG EVIDENCE

FIRM GROUND
Intelligence

Ambiguous
information

Strongly
held view

Unclear or
no view

Assumption-led
information

Missing
information

WEAK or NO EVIDENCE

Figure 6.2: The discrepancy matrix. Reprinted with permission from Wonnacott J (2014) *Developing and Supporting Effective Staff Supervision*. Pavilion Publishing and Media.

Case example: Harry & Joe

Harry is seven and in Year 2, Joe, his brother, is five and in Reception class. They have two younger sisters, Mya who is four and in the nursery attached to the school and Alice who is two. All four children live with their parents; the mother brings the children to school, the father has never been seen at the school. The children's school attendance has reached a level of 60% unauthorised absence. When Harry was in Year 1 he briefly lived with his maternal grandmother and achieved 100% attendance and was noticeably better prepared for school, with clean uniform and his reading book every day. He also appeared happier and ready to learn. The explanation given at that time was that the mother had gone to a refuge fleeing domestic abuse, she subsequently returned to her partner.

Joe, after a term in Reception, is prone to getting into fights with other children about sharing toys or activities. He responds well to the teaching assistant who takes him out and does a range of physical activities. Harry rarely has his reading book with him, his pattern of attendance makes it hard for him to retain what he is being taught and he often appears to be in his own world in class, unable to make friends with the other children. Neither child is assessed as learning and their imagery and play is violent in content.

Attempts by the head teacher to get the parents into school to discuss the children do not succeed although when there is free food (donated by arrangement with the local supermarket instead of being thrown away) the mother will usually attend and so the DSL or DDSL try to make sure they are available to talk about the children then. The school ensure there is always extra food available so that Harry and Joe are offered breakfast in addition to lunch when they attend school.

In analysing this information the quadrants could be filled in in the following way.

Firm ground (where there is evidence which fits with the professional viewpoint of those filling in the matrix).

- Attendance rates – currently 60% unauthorised absence.
- Mother always attends when a text goes out for free food.
- Boys complain of being hungry on arrival at school.
- Known history of domestic abuse between the parents.
- Harry's attendance and readiness to learn was much better when cared for by his grandmother.
- The boys' behaviour in class and concerns about learning.
- Parents non-attendance at formal consultative meetings.

Ambiguous information (where the evidence may be strong but the professional view on it is yet to be determined)

■ Not known why the parents do not attend the consultative meetings.

■ Unclear whether the parents are able to read and help with the children's learning. Offers of help from a school teaching assistant have not been taken up.

■ The nursery have passed on their concerns about Mya making the transition to Reception. She is currently not toilet trained and has fewer words than would be expected at her age.

Missing information (this is a great section, what information don't you know that might make a difference if you did know it?)

■ Father is not known and has never knowingly been seen at school.

■ Parental views about education.

■ Levels of financial difficulty/housing arrangements. Family refused the pre-school home visit.

■ What the reasons for the children's absence are.

Assumption-led information (what assumptions are being made and is there any evidence for them? Do the assumptions need to be discounted because they are in fact, bias?)

■ There is ongoing violence in the home.

■ That the children may be being injured and this could be why they are not in school.

■ That the children's presentations are indicative of being traumatised, Joe is in fight mode and Harry is withdrawing.

■ The children may have specific learning difficulties.

■ That the children are being under-fed and may be at risk of neglect.

■ That the mother has learning difficulties and may be struggling to feed the children.

The quadrants do not have to be filled in in the order that has happened here and, in fact, it is likely that over the course of a discussion there will be a flitting backwards and forwards. The discussion can allow the making of hypothesis and testing out what actions should be taken as a result of the discussion. In the above example it is likely that there will be more information coming out which will clarify whether this is a safeguarding referral for neglect and emotional abuse, a referral around attendance, a request for educational learning assessments or a further plan of action within the school to gather more information about the impact on the children of what is happening in their lives.

Thinking point

■ Consider a situation at your school concerning either a student or staff member about which you or a colleague has expressed some disquiet.

■ Try the matrix to see whether it offers you any clarity of thinking. It is usually helpful to do this with at least one other person to challenge your perspective.

Conclusion

For supervision to be effective in school settings there has to be committed support from the senior leadership team. This chapter has offered a range of ideas about what effective supervision might look like in schools. It starts with a reflective, reflexive supervisor, alert and responsive to the needs of the staff and interested in the well-being of students. Effective supervisors are committed to looking after themselves and aware of the impact of their behaviour on others. The chapter has included suggestions to increase this awareness and tools to use with staff whether in individual or group supervision. The next chapter will look at ways of supporting the leadership team to embed a supervision culture.

Chapter 7: Establishing a culture of supervision

Introduction

Supervision of staff with the meaning ascribed in this guide is a new concept to education and school settings. Despite being part of the statutory framework for Early Years since 2012, it has rarely been offered in schools, even to those for whom it is mandated; nursery and Reception staff. Increasingly the guidance *Working Together to Safeguard Children* (Department for Education, 2015; 2017) speaks of staff in schools involved in safeguarding children being offered 'supervision and support' in such work. For supervision to be effective it needs to be part of the culture in schools that reinforces and builds on expectations about supervision. This chapter looks at how to build a culture in which effective supervision can flourish. Using the Appreciative Inquiry Framework of what is working well and how it can be improved provides tools to audit supervisory practice and ideas for establishing the culture effectively.

How supervision is essential to safe practice

Supervision as outlined in Chapter 1 is part of maintaining safe practices within the school. In thinking about the importance of supervision and establishing a culture of supervision it is worth restating some of the observations from earlier chapters. In Chapter 2 the impact of supervision on the key stakeholders (4Ss) was investigated. This is the centre of the integrated model, the people who benefit from effective supervision. The benefit to the students emphasised their learning and development, stimulated by high quality, consistent teaching provided within an enabling, safe environment. Staff developed their own skills, shared their worries about their own or others' practice and were supported in their role to achieve the Teacher's Standards. For the school, the importance of students being safe, learning well and being respectful cannot be underestimated, as parents ultimately make decisions about whether they will continue to support the school, determined by their view about the safety and well-being of their child. Therefore key to the success of the school is keeping students happy by having a safe environment and skilled staff.

Supervision should be part of the method for achieving these aims. Staff should be encouraged to report their observations, their feedback about their own and others' practice in a way that encourages transparency and trust. These are factors that protect children in group environments. Green (2012, p.186) summarises the main factors of a safe organisation providing group care to children below:

'1. *Robust recruitment procedures.*
2. *Written codes of conduct.*
3. *Expectation that staff follow codes of conduct.*
4. *Induction and regular training review.*
5. *SUPERVISION, policy and carried out.*
6. *Know about whistle blowing policy and how to use it.*
7. *Prompt and robust action when concerns raised.*
8. *Work closely with multi-disciplinary team colleagues and accept their advice when needed.*
9. *Understand difference between criminal behaviour and what falls outside the code of conduct.*
10. *Follow disciplinary procedures appropriately.*
11. *Ensure procedures and process is fair.'*

Thinking point

Review the indicators of a safe organisation above.

■ What is already in place where you work?

■ What is missing?

■ Would students, staff, parents and governors agree with your assessment?

Safe organisations provide supervision to and of their staff

Having stated the importance of supervision to safeguarding children, it is imperative that the culture is reinforced by the senior leadership team in the school. In thinking about how to establish a culture of supervision in settings where this is an unfamiliar concept, the following diagram, Figure 7.1, has been used. It is designed to demonstrate the process of getting supervision embedded into the culture and practice of each school.

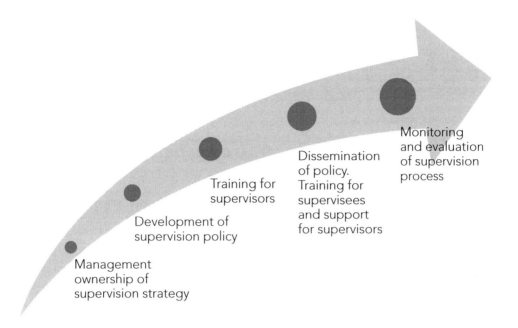

Figure 7.1: Developing a supervision culture

Management ownership of the supervision strategy and developing supervision policy

In previous chapters there has been discussion about some of the challenges presented in making supervision a reality in schools. The direction of travel would suggest that there will be an expectation that supervision of staff, especially those involved in safeguarding, is likely to be strongly encouraged in newer guidance following on from some of the Serious Case Reviews involving the abuse of children by school staff (Wonnacott *et al*, 2018). Tertiary education staff are expected and inspected on being supervised as well as those in Early Years settings, so not including primary and secondary education staff increasingly looks like an oversight.

While acknowledging that there may still remain some resistance, nevertheless it is likely that schools will be seeking advice about how to provide supervision to staff and the best ways of doing it. Understanding the explicit link with safer practice and keeping students of all ages safeguarded begins to shift resistance. Supervision facilitates discussion about staff behaviour and promotes transparent cultures which also safeguard staff.

The leadership role requires the senior leadership team to sell the benefits of supervision within their school. The importance of supervision being a safe space to reflect on what staff have done well and to think about how to improve. An opportunity to identify learning needs. The space to reflect on the impact working with students can have. This guide provides ideas about how this can be done. However in order for this to be effective it is helpful to have a policy which makes clear what the senior leadership team see as the purpose and aim of supervision for their particular school. Below is a template document that can be used to begin the process. As with all the templates included in this guide it is intended as a starting point for discussion with the key people who need to make supervision effective in each setting. Like all policies and procedures none are effective unless they make sense to staff in their school.

Introduction to supervision policy

'Everyone who comes in contact with children and their families and carers has a role to play in safeguarding children … School and college staff are particularly important as they are in a position to identify concerns early, provide help for children, and prevent concerns escalating… [designated safeguarding leads] *will provide support to staff members to carrying out their safeguarding duties and* [who] *will liaise closely with other services such as children's social care.'* (Department for Education, 2016)

Supervision is a method of ensuring staff are clear on their responsibilities and supported in their roles to safeguard students. This policy is based on the premise that the supervision of staff is an integral part of the day-to-day business of our school and supplements other management practices. It will occur both formally and in other forums including informal discussions and group settings. In these forums, the process of supervision should be informed by the standards set out within this document.

[This school] recognises that:

- Staff supervision is integral to the effective delivery of services.
- The quality of staff supervision impacts on outcomes for students.
- The delivery of supervision must be a priority task within the school.
- Staff have the right to receive regular formal supervision from supervisors who have received appropriate training and are supported within their supervisory role.
- All staff have a responsibility to participate in supervision and attend formal sessions.
- The process of supervision is shared responsibility: staff and their supervisors are expected to contribute to the effectiveness of the process and the school has a responsibility to facilitate a culture which supports the process.

Scope

[To be developed and agreed within the school depending upon management structure.]

Definition – what is supervision?

[To be developed and agreed within the school but could be based on the definition below:]

For the purposes of this policy supervision is defined as a process by which one staff member is given responsibility by the school to work with another member of staff in order to meet certain school, professional and personal objectives in order to promote positive outcomes for students. The objectives are:

1. Competent, accountable performance. [Managerial function]

2. Continuing professional development. [Educational/development function]

3. Personal support. [Supportive function]

4. Linking the individual to the organisation. [Mediation function]

(Definition taken and adapted from Morrison (2005) *Staff Supervision in Social Care.* Brighton: Pavilion Publishing & Media).

The process of supervision is supported by the development of a relationship between supervisors and supervisees which provides a safe environment to support the staff member and facilitate reflection, challenge and critical thinking.

Statement of expectations

[To be developed and agreed within the school but could be based on the paragraphs below:]

The school will:

1. Prioritise supervision as an important activity within the school.

2. Ensure that all staff who come within the scope of this policy have a named supervisor who also has line management responsibility for their work and welfare.

3. Provide training and ongoing development opportunities for supervisors.

4. Ensure appropriate space is provided for meetings, whether individually or in groups.

5. Regularly evaluate the quality of supervision being provided.

Supervisors will:

1. Ensure the delivery of one-to-one/group supervision sessions at a frequency in line with this policy.
2. Ensure that supervision is recorded in line with the expectations set out within this policy.
3. Ensure that the prime focus of supervision is to safeguard students' well-being and maintaining public trust (Teacher's Standards, 2013).
4. Use the supervision agreement as the basis for the development of a relationship where supervisees can be supported in their work and reflect on their practice.
5. Ensure the supervisee is clear about how to raise any concerns about the quality of supervision being received.
6. Use the supervisory process to learn from good practice and give constructive feedback to promote professional development.
7. Address performance concerns as they arise and work positively with the supervisee to improve practice.
8. Take responsibility for their personal development as a supervisor and use their own supervision to reflect on their supervisory practice.

Supervisees will:

1. Take responsibility for attending one-to-one supervision or group sessions as set out in their supervision agreement.
2. Prepare adequately for supervision and take an active part in the process.
3. Take responsibility for raising any concerns they may have about the quality of the supervisory relationship with the supervisor or, if this is not possible, the third party named within the supervision agreement.

Method of delivery

[To be developed and agreed within the school but could be based on the paragraphs below:]

A relationship between a supervisor and supervisee is fundamental to the supervisory process and supervision will take place in a variety of settings and circumstances.

A formal supervision session, whether in a group or one-to-one is at the heart of the process and staff should receive regular supervision.

Ad hoc supervision is the dialogue that takes place between a supervisor and supervisee as the need arises. This should be available to all staff but is not a substitute for formal group/one-to-one supervision. The value of ad hoc supervision is that it is an important way of supporting staff, improving performance, keeping pace with change and ensuring that the school's requirements are met. It should be recorded in line with these procedures.

Frequency

[To be developed and agreed within the school.]

The supervision agreement

The development of a productive supervisory relationship starts with:

- Clarity about roles and responsibilities and the school's requirements.
- Building rapport, understanding each other's perspective and any factors that might affect the process.
- Acknowledging that effective supervision may not always be comfortable and exploring how power, authority and differences of opinion may be negotiated.

This process should be captured within the written agreement and it is the responsibility of supervisors to ensure that an agreement is in place for every supervisee, using the school's template. This agreement should be signed by both parties and placed in the supervisee's file.

The written agreement is a working tool and should be reviewed at least once a year.

Supervision process and content

[To be developed and agreed within the school but could refer to the four functions of supervision and the use of the supervision cycle.]

Recording supervision

[To be developed and agreed within the school.]

Monitoring and review

[To be developed and agreed within the school – including how supervisee's feedback on the process will be obtained.]

Thinking point

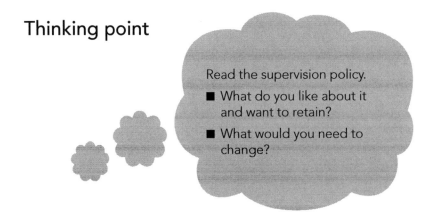

Read the supervision policy.
- What do you like about it and want to retain?
- What would you need to change?

Contained within the supervision policy are the various chapters of the guide that define the integrated model. The definition of supervision is that used in Chapter 1. The rim of the model includes the four aspects of supervision (management, mediation, development and support). The purpose of supervision and expectations about its functions need to be clear within the supervision policy. They should follow through into each agreement between supervisor and supervisee. It is useful if these elements form part of a recording template too as a further reminder of the purpose of having supervision. Therefore to successfully embed a supervision culture there should be a supervision policy, linking to an agreement and recording template suitable for each school. The templates are expected to be used flexibly for the specific needs of each staff member and able to reflect the needs of students in the school.

For supervision to be effective, it is essential that all participants in the process understand why they are having supervision. Expectations on supervisors and supervisees are explicit and both parties agree with one another how they will make supervision work for them and what to do if it does not. The focus is on schools that enable all students to learn and develop in their own unique way. It may be helpful to reference the Teachers' Standards in the policy too.

Alongside the Teachers' Standards is a recognition of the reach of supervision to benefit the people who are at the centre of the integrated model (Chapter 2). The four stakeholders also need to be referenced in the policy i.e. the 4Ss; the students, the staff, the school, the external stakeholders (families and other agencies the provider works with).

How supervision is going to work, the methods and frequency will include a discussion about the supervisory cycle from Chapter 3. In order to maintain professional development staff need opportunities to participate in all four elements of the supervisory cycle; experience, reflection, analysis and action planning. This links the centre of the model to its rim. The more staff and supervisors understand about the learning cycle, its application to supervision including the need for each element, the more able they are to use these processes to achieve better outcomes. Staff will find it helpful to understand how they learn (which part of the learning cycle they prefer to join) as well as why each element is needed.

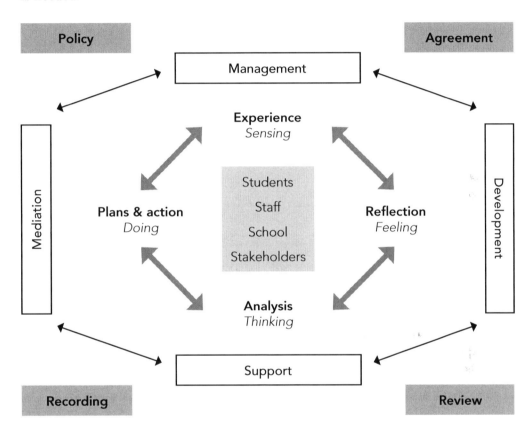

Figure 7.2: The integrated model of supervision. Adapted with permission from Morrison T (2005) *Staff Supervision in Social Care* (3rd edition). Brighton: Pavilion Publishing.

Each school will work out how frequently formal supervision happens. As a guide, replacing the termly performance appraisal with supervision each half term and having an annual appraisal might be one idea. Some schools in the pilot decided to offer fortnightly, brief, individual supervision amplified by group supervision each half term. Some staff, especially when they are new to the school, role or are inexperienced, may require more frequent supervision with a more directive stance. Perhaps supervision could be linked to the induction process and contribute to the performance appraisal about whether a member of staff is confirmed in their post (see Chapter 1 for a discussion of what is performance appraisal and what belongs to supervision). Those who are experienced and have been well supported may manage with half-termly frequency and should be capable of being more self-directive in their needs (see discussion in Chapter 4 about using coaching in authoritative supervisory practice). These timings would be an advisory minimal expectation of supervision.

Development of supervision policy using Appreciative Inquiry models of change

Appreciative Inquiry (AI) is a theory developed by Cooperrider and Srivastva (1987) looking to bring about change by building on what already works well. It has been adapted for research and organisational purposes (Martins, 2014). A good starting point is to ask questions about the current situation before changing anything and this is the basis of the AI approach, just asking the first question brings about change. AI is a phased model of engaging a range of stakeholders in a process of change and therefore fits well with the challenges facing education settings implementing changes of practice. Importantly the expectation is on collaboration from everyone with any interest in the issue, so that multiple perspectives are considered. AI also understands that how adults and students relate to each other is significant.

Applying these ideas to introducing supervision, for example, 'What is appreciated about how supervision is working at present in school?', the senior leadership team may start by asking a series of questions:

■ How do supervisees and supervisors feel about supervision?

■ How do parents feel about the teaching and how their child is learning?

■ How do parents feel about the information they receive from school?

It could be helpful to involve governors and other stakeholders in the process of evaluating the current situation. Students may also be consulted.
Noticing and paying attention to where there is consensus on what is working well is an important part of the AI model, paying attention to success builds confidence in the process of change. It is worth spending time gaining views about what is working well. Change has a tendency to focus on negative elements and valuing what is working well about the current situation genuinely engages staff in wanting to improve as what they are already doing is appreciated.

Thinking points

■ What about how the school and staff are being managed is working well for you?

■ What about supervision is working well for you – as supervisor and as supervisee?

■ What is not working well?

Recognising that change is not going to happen for the sake of it will embolden people to say what they would like to see done differently and thereby move into the next phase. The first phase may have been done individually, for example through questionnaires; the next phase will probably involve joining together in some way to imagine a different way of doing things. It is important to identify who the key people are to begin the process of envisaging the future; there should ideally be representation from key stakeholders not just the managerial team. In this instance collective input generally produces better results.

Once the end goal is identified, for example, 'how will this school know that supervision is working effectively?', the key stakeholders need to find a way of deciding how to reach it. Originally Cooperrider used terms like dreaming, design and discovery for these parts of the process. Although those names can be off-putting, it is useful occasionally to be reminded that dreaming of a future helps with designing the processes by which it is reached. What would it look like to have an effective supervision policy and culture in the school, and what steps do we need to get there? In every situation there are unintended consequences, which is where the AI model offers flexibility, as the final process (discovery) recognises that while the design may envisage reaching a certain place (dream), there could be future unknown situations which need to be taken into account and adjusted for. What ends up happening may differ from what seemed possible. The essential component in an AI model for change is recognising the fluidity with which human beings interact with their environment. This differs from linear experimental design models that expect outcomes that conform to the expectations identified at the start of the process.

On the next page there is an audit tool which could be a useful starting point in identifying what challenges exist around supervision. Schools will be in differing places on these processes and this is once again a suggestion for discussion within the senior leadership team in each school or across trusts.

Thinking points

- Using the audit tool, what is in place and working well?
- What do you think the most important thing to do next is?
- Why?
- Who else do you need to consult with?

Developing a culture of supervision: an audit tool

	Yes	No	In development	Action needed
As a management team are we clear about why supervision is important in our school?				
Have we discussed the model and style of supervision that we wish to promote?				
Are we clear about the practical arrangements such as frequency and how supervision will be recorded?				
Is a written supervision policy in place?				
Is it clear how the supervision policy fits with other policies including safeguarding, staff appraisal and personal development plans?				
Have we identified the minimum training that supervisors should have before they start supervising?				
Is there a process in place for disseminating the supervision policy to both established and new staff?				
Is there training for supervisees on how to make the best use of supervision?				
What support is in place for supervisors? Are there robust supervision arrangements for them too?				
Are there plans for the ongoing development of supervisory skills?				
Do we have a system in place for evaluating the quality of supervision including obtaining feedback from supervisees?				

Once the supervision policy has been worked out by the leadership team, there is then a process of identifying how supervisors will be trained and supported in their role. Such training impacts on building a culture that gets shared with other staff, explaining the purpose of supervision and assisting in training supervisees so that they prepare for, and make good use of supervision. There then need to be processes which evaluate the quality and effectiveness of supervision, getting responses from supervisees and supervisors about the impact supervision is having on confidence and competence. By this point the expectation would be that supervision has become embedded within the everyday practice of the school.

This chapter has reiterated the role of supervision in group child care settings as a protective factor in keeping schools safe for children. The link between supervision and safeguarding practice is an important one that the governors and senior leadership team need to make sure their staff understand. Following on from this was a discussion about reinforcing the centrality of supervision by having a supervision policy. An audit tool of supervisory practice offered a framework to evaluate and develop the culture of supervision.

Final thoughts

Supervision is increasingly expected in education, especially for staff involved in safeguarding. Making supervision really effective can however be a challenge and this guide has set out ideas and tools to help the senior leadership team establish and maintain good supervision practices. As Chapter 6 identified, good supervision does not take place in isolation, and will thrive in healthy settings where the focus is always on the needs of the students. Supervision needs promotion and endorsement by the Senior Leadership Team as a key aspect of the school.

One important question remains: who sustains, develops and supervises the supervisors? There needs to be arrangements in place for support and oversight of the work of those people who have responsibility for delivery of effective supervision, perhaps in arrangements with partnership schools in trusts or locally connected to one another.

Supervisors need to be adequately trained to do the job, since un-trained supervisors are unlikely to have the knowledge or confidence to deliver the type of effective supervision described in this guide. However, training alone is not enough. In order to sustain supervision beyond an initial training course, supervisors need the opportunity to stand back and reflect on their work, including the challenges of providing supervision to their staff team. How this is achieved may vary but must be an important question for all those responsible for educating students in school settings.

Perhaps the last words of all should come from a Teaching Assistant from one of the pilot schools:

"supervision to be made a requirement not a suggestion."

Appendices

Appendix 1: Supervision functions

The following lists are not exhaustive, but they may help supervisors to consider how far their supervisory practice delivers across all four functions of supervision.

The support function checklist

The aims of the support function are:

- To validate staff both as a professional and as a person.

- To create a safe climate, staff to look at their practice and its impact on them as a person.

- To clarify the boundaries between support, counselling, consultation and to clarify the limits of confidentiality in supervision.

- To explore issues about discrimination, in a safe setting.

- To support staff who are subject to any form of abuse either from students, parents or from other colleagues, whether this be physical, psychological or discriminatory.

- To monitor the overall health and emotional functioning of staff, especially about the effects of stress.

- To debrief staff and give the staff member permission to talk about feelings, especially fear, anger, sadness, repulsion or helplessness.

- To help staff to explore emotional blocks to the work.

- To help staff reflect on difficulties in peer relationships to assist the staff member in resolving conflict.

- To clarify when the staff member should be advised to seek external counselling, and its relationship with the monitoring of performance.

The management function checklist

The aims of the management function are to ensure:

- The staff member understands their role and responsibilities.

- The staff member is clear as to the limits and use of their own role, that of the school and the role of the statutory authority.

- The purpose of the supervision is clear.

- The staff member is given an appropriate workload.

- Time-management expectations of staff are clear and checked.

- The staff member acts as a positive member of the team.

- The staff member understands the functions of other agencies and relates appropriately to them.

- The staff member receives regular formal appraisal.

- The overall quality of the staff member's performance is measured.

- The policies and procedures of the school are understood and followed.

- Work is reviewed regularly in accordance with the school and legal requirements.

- Action plans are formulated and carried out within the expectations of the school and statutory responsibilities.

- The basis of decisions and professional judgements are clear to you and staff members and written explicitly in the student's or employee's records.

- Records are maintained according to the school's policies.

- Each staff member knows when their line manager or head teacher expects to be consulted.

The development function checklist

The aims of this function are to assist the development of:

- Teacher's professional competence.

- An appreciation and assessment of the staff member's knowledge base, skills, and individual contribution to the school.

- An understanding of each staff member's value base in relation to race, gender, sexuality, religion, disability etc. and its impact on his/her work.

- An understanding of the staff member's preferred learning style and blocks to learning.

- An assessment of the staff member's training and development needs and how they can be met.

- The staff member's capacity to set professional goals.

- Access to professional consultation in areas outside the line manager's knowledge/experience.

- The staff member's ability to reflect on their work and interaction with students, parents, peers and other agencies.

- Regular and constructive feedback to the staff member on all aspects of their performance.

- The staff member's ability to generalise learning and to increase their commitment and capacity to ongoing professional development.

- The staff member's capacity for self-appraisal, and the ability to learn constructively from significant experiences or difficulties.

- A relationship in which the staff member provides constructive feedback to the line manager and both can learn.

The mediation function checklist

The aims of the mediation function are to:

- Negotiate and clarify the school's remit.

- Brief the leadership team about resource deficits or implications.

- Allocate resources in the most efficient way.

- Represent staff needs to the leadership team.

- Initiate, clarify or contribute to policy formulation.

- Consult and brief other staff members about developments or information about the school.

- Mediate or advocate between teachers, teaching assistants and others within the school or with outside agencies.

- Represent or accompany staff members in work with other agencies e.g. child protection case conferences.

- Involve staff members in decision making.

- Deal sensitively, but clearly, with complaints about staff.

- Assist and coach staff members, where appropriate, through complaints procedures.

Appendix 2: Possible questions for supervision

Focusing on experience

Here the emphasis is on facilitating an accurate and detailed recall of events since a partial description of the situation will undermine the rest of the cycle. We can be assisted to recall more than we think we know if the right questions are asked.

- How do you see your role with this student/class?

- How do think others (professionals and family) see your role?

- What did you expect to happen?

- What happened?

- What reactions did you notice to what you said/did?

- What surprised or puzzled you?

- What struck you? What were the key moments?

- What words, non-verbal communication, smells, sounds, images struck you?

- What did you notice about yourself/ this student /other students in the class/ other staff in the room?

- What was hard to observe?

- What went according to plan? What didn't happen?

- What changes or choices did you make?

- What did you say, notice or do immediately after the event?

These questions can be enhanced by using other methods, such as learning walks, video or audio recording, observation, learning diaries, or incident logs. Eco maps/ genograms might also be helpful at this point.

Focusing on reflection

Here the emphasis is on eliciting feelings, partly because they bring out further information, or may reveal our underlying attitudes and assumptions. They may also give clues to other personal factors complicating the staff member's experience. Reflection helps the staff member make links between the current situation and his/her prior experiences, skills and knowledge.

- What feelings did you bring into the session?

- What is your gut feeling about this student?

- Describe the range of feelings you had in the lesson?

- What did the lesson or this student(s) remind you of?

- What previous work, processes, skills, knowledge are relevant here?

- Where have you encountered similar processes?

- What assumptions might you be making? For example, assumptions related to race, culture, age, gender, sexuality, ability.

- Does this situation challenge your feelings about acceptable/unacceptable behaviour?

- Where and when did you feel most or least comfortable?

- What feelings were you left with – does this always happen after being in these kinds of lessons/classes?

- What metaphor or analogy would you describe your experiences of working with this situation?

- What was left unfinished?

Other methods to assist reflection include role play, sculpting, art work to draw out feelings and perceptions, further reflection on genograms and eco-maps to draw out context, roles and patterns.

Focusing on analysis

Here the emphasis is on analysis, probing the meanings that the supervisee and the student (s) attribute to the situation, consideration of other explanations, the identification of what is known or understood, and the areas for further assessment.

- Taking account of your feelings – what does this tell us about what the students may be feeling in this situation?
- How do you explain or understand what happened?
- How would this have been different if the student had been female/black/disabled, etc.?
- Did power relations shift – if so how and why?
- What went well, or not well, and why?
- How far did this lesson confirm or challenge your previous understanding or hypothesis?
- What new information emerged?
- What theory, training, research, policy, values might help you make sense of what happened?
- How else might you have managed the lesson/situation?
- What are the current needs, risks, strengths in this situation?
- What is unknown?
- What conclusions are you drawing from this work so far?
- How do you now define your role in this situation?
- How would the students define your role?
- What expectations does the school have of your role?

Other methods to assist analysis include sharing articles, references, case presentations, external speakers, attending in-service training, group supervision and action learning sets.

Focusing on action plans

The focus here is on translating the analysis into planning, preparation and action. This includes the identification of outcomes and success criteria as well as consideration of potential complications and contingency plans.

■ In light of the reflection and analysis we have done, what is your overall summary of where things are at, and what needs to be done next?

■ Can you identify what you are, and what you are not responsible for in managing this situation?

■ What training, co-work and support needs have been raised for you?

■ What information needs to be obtained from others before proceeding?

■ What are your aims in the next phase of work?

■ What is urgent and essential?

■ What would be desirable?

■ What is negotiable and what is non-negotiable in this situation?

■ What would be a successful outcome from your perspective/the student/other students/school or key agencies?

■ What might be your strategy for the next contact with the student/their family/the class and other professionals?

■ What are the possible best or worst responses from the student, the class or families of the students?

■ What contingency plans do you need – what is the bottom line?

■ Where do you feel more or less confident?

■ How can you prepare for the next steps – prepared scripts for commonly occurring situations or for difficult conversations, mental rehearsal, flip chart map, reading, co-worker discussion?

■ What can I do that would be helpful at this stage?

■ When does feedback and debriefing need to take place?

■ What restorative sessions are required?

■ Are there any safety issues for you/others?

■ What can be done to minimise any dangers?

Other methods may include role play, co-work planning, care planning, contacting other agencies involved.

References

Asthana A & Boycott-Owen M (2018) 'Epidemic of stress' blamed for 3,750 teachers on long-term sick leave. *The Guardian* **11 January**.

Bombèr L & Hughes D (2013) *Settling to Learn: Settling troubled pupils to learn, why relationships matter in school*. London: Worth Publishing.

Cain S (2011) *Quiet: The power of introverts in a world that can't stop talking*. London: Penguin.

Cooperrider D & Srivastva S (1987) Appreciative inquiry in organizational life. In R. Woodman and W. Pasmore (Eds) *Research in Organizational Change and Development Volume 1* (pp129–169). Bingley, UK: Emerald Publishing.

Department for Education (2013) *Teachers' Standards: Guidance for school leaders, school staff and governing bodies* [online]. Available at: www.gov.uk/government/publications/teachers-standards (accessed April 2018).

Department for Education (2015) *Working Together to Safeguard Children: A guide to inter-agency working to safeguard and promote the welfare of children*. Available at: https://assets.publishing. service.gov.uk/government/uploads/system/uploads/attachment_data/file/592101/Working_Together_to_Safeguard_Children_20170213.pdf (accessed May 2018).

Department for Education (2018) *Keeping Children Safe in Education: Statutory guidance for schools and colleges* [online]. Available at: https://consult.education.gov.uk/safeguarding-in-schools-team/keeping-children-safe-in-education/supporting_documents/Keeping%20Children%20Safe%20in%20Education%20Proposed%20Revisions.pdf (accessed May 2018).

Department for Education (2017) *Statutory Framework for the Early Years Foundation Stage: Setting the standards for learning, development and care for children from birth to five*. Available at: https://assets.publishing.service.gov.uk/government/uploads/system/uploads/attachment_data/file/596629/EYFS_STATUTORY_FRAMEWORK_2017.pdf (accessed May 2018).

Dix P (2017) *When the Adults Change Everything Changes: Seismic shifts in school behaviour*. Wales: Independent Thinking Press.

Downey M (2003) *Effective Coaching: Lessons from the coach's coach (2nd edition)*. London: Engage Learning.

Erooga M (2012) *Creating Safer Organisations: Practical steps to prevent the abuse of children by those working with them*. Chichester: Wiley-Blackwell.

Erooga M (2018) *Protecting Children and Adults from Abuse after Savile: What organisations and institutions need to do*. London: Jessica Kingsley Publishers.

Gerhardt S (2004) *Why Love Matters: How affection shapes a baby's brain*. Hove: Routledge.

Goleman D (1995) *Emotional Intelligence: Why it can matter more than IQ*. London: Bloomsbury Publishing.

Grant L & Kinman G (2014) *Developing Resilience for Social Work Practice*. London: Palgrave Macmillan.

Green J (2012) Avoiding and Managing Allegations against Staff. In: M Erooga (Ed.) *Creating Safer Organisations: Practical steps to prevent the abuse of children by those working with them*. Chichester: Wiley-Blackwell.

Hay J (1995) *Transformational Mentoring: Creating developmental alliances for changing organisational culture*. New York: McGraw-Hill Education.

Harris C (2018) 'The only sticking plaster holding schools together? The army of teaching assistants' [online]. Available at: https://www.tes.com/news/school-news/breaking-views/only-sticking-plaster-holding-schools-together-army-teaching (accessed April 2018).

ITV News (2018) *Shocking scale of sexual abuse at UK boarding schools revealed by ITV documentary* [online] Available at: http://www.itv.com/news/2018-02-18/shocking-scale-of-sexual-abuse-at-uk-boarding-schools-revealed-by-itv-documentary/ (accessed April 2018).

Kolb DA (1988) *Experiential Learning: Experience as the source of learning and development.* London: Pearson Education.

Lambley, S, Marrable T & Lawson H (2013) *Practice Enquiry into Supervision in a Variety of Adult Care Settings Where There are Health and Social Care Practitioners Working Together.* Social Care Institute for Excellence (SCIE).

Martins C (2014) *Appreciative Inquiry in Child Protection: Identifying and promoting good practice and creating a learning culture practice tool.* Devon: Research in Practice.

Morrison T (2005) *Staff Supervision in Social Care (3rd edition).* Brighton: Pavilion Publishing & Media.

Morrison T (2007) Emotional intelligence, emotion and social work: context, characteristics, complications and contribution. *British Journal of Social Work* **37** 245–263.

Rock & Siegel (2012) *Healthy Mind Platter* [online]. Available at: http://m.drdansiegel.com/resources/healthy_mind_platter/ (accessed April 2018).

Sturt P & Wonnacott J (2016) *Supervision for Early Years Workers: A guide for early years professionals about the requirements of supervision.* Brighton: Pavilion Publishing & Media Ltd.

Sunderland M (2007) *What Every Parent Needs to Know: The incredible effects of love, nurture and play on your child's development.* London: DK.

Wonnacott J (2012) *Mastering Social Work Supervision.* London: Jessica Kingsley Publishers.

Wonnacott, J (2014) *Developing and Supporting Effective Staff Supervision.* Brighton: Pavilion Publishing & Media Ltd.

Wonnacott J, Foster J & Shaw H (2018) After Savile: Implications for education settings. In M Erooga (Ed.) *Protecting Children and Adults from Abuse after Savile: What organisations and institutions need to do.* London: Jessica Kingsley Publishers.

Other useful resources from Pavilion Publishing

Supervision for Early Years Workers: A guide for early years professionals about the requirements of supervision
Jane Wonnacott and Penny Sturt

This guide will support early years providers in the delivery of effective staff supervision. Although the Early Years Foundation Stage (EYFS) sets out the framework of expectations in relation to supervision, there are still many differing ideas as to what good supervision looks like in practice and how this can be provided by a busy early years manager. This guide address these fundamental questions:

- Why is supervision so important?
- What are the core components of supervision?
- How can a supervisor and supervisee work together to make supervision effective?

Available at: https://www.pavpub.com/supervision-for-early-years-workers/

Developing and Supporting Effective Staff Supervision: A training pack to support the delivery of staff supervision training for those working with vulnerable children, adults and their families
Jane Wonnacott, developed from materials by Tony Morrison

This training pack draws on the core concepts in Tony Morrison's *Staff Supervision in Social Care* and demonstrates how they can be used to train staff to deliver sound and effective supervision that makes a real difference to service users.

This training pack is for use by experienced trainers who are well grounded in supervision practice and theory. It focuses on training supervisors to deliver one-to-one supervision and its flexible structure enables trainers to design their own bespoke training programmes.

Through group and pair work, participants are actively encouraged to examine and explore their own practice and work together to extend their thinking and improve their skills as supervisors. This pack goes beyond merely teaching theory and actively encourages professional reflection and development.

Available at: https://www.pavpub.com/developing-and-supporting-effective-staffsupervision-training-pack/

Staff Supervision in Social Care: Making a real difference for staff and service users
Tony Morrison

This substantial manual contains vital information for anyone involved in supervising, coaching, mentoring or assessing trainees, students and staff involved in delivering or managing services in health, social care, education welfare and community justice settings. The resource contains accessible theory and frameworks with illustrations, examples, diagrams and summaries, photocopiable exercises, checklists and questionnaires.

Available at: https://www.pavpub.com/staff-supervision-in-social-care/

Strength to Strength: A facilitator's guide to preparing supervisees, students and trainees for supervision
Tony Morrison

A flexible, session-based resource for facilitators to inform, enhance and accelerate the capacity of supervisees to make maximum use of the supervision process. Improving the contribution to the supervision process, this resource contains guidance for facilitators, development tools and exercises, checklists and additional resources. It contains vital information for trainers and supervisors of trainees, students and staff involved in delivering or managing services in health, social care, education welfare and community justice settings.

Available at: https://www.pavpub.com/strength-to-strength/